ICT and Pr

This book is for teachers who are looking for interesting and practical ways to incorporate ICT into their daily lesson plans. The book shows how ICT can be used as a tool for mathematics, but more importantly how its proper use can enhance the mathematics being taught. The authors cover all current aspects of ICT and mathematics, including:

■ Databases
■ Spreadsheets
■ LOGO and the use of floor turtles and control technology
■ Handling of resources including interactive whiteboards
■ Management of ICT within the classroom
■ How ICT can be used to present mathematical topics and links to other areas of the curriculum

With plenty of suggestions on how to use the software and hardware described in the book, this is a highly illustrated and useful resource for all primary teachers, particularly subject co-ordinators for ICT and mathematics. *ICT and Primary Mathematics* will also be of interest to students on PGCE and Initial Teacher Training courses.

John Williams has worked in primary education for many years as a class teacher, headteacher, advisor for science and technology and more recently as Senior Lecturer in Higher Education at Anglia Polytechnic University. **Nick Easingwood** is Senior Lecturer for ICT in Education and ICT Co-ordinator for the School of Education at Anglia Polytechnic University. John Williams and Nick Easingwood are also authors of *ICT and Primary Science*.

ICT and Primary Mathematics

John Williams and
Nick Easingwood

RoutledgeFalmer
Taylor & Francis Group

LONDON AND NEW YORK

First published 2004
by RoutledgeFalmer
2 Park Square, Milton Park, Abingdon, Oxfordshire OX14 4RN

Simultaneously published in the USA and Canada
by RoutledgeFalmer
270 Madison Avenue, New York, NY 10016

RoutledgeFalmer is an imprint of the Taylor & Francis Group

© 2004 John Williams and Nick Easingwood

Typeset in Melior by
HWA Text and Data Management, Tunbridge Wells
Printed and bound in Great Britain by
TJ International Ltd, Padstow, Cornwall

British Library Cataloguing in Publication Data
A catalogue record for this book is available from the
British Library

Library of Congress Cataloging in Publication Data
Williams, John, 1936–
  ICT & primary mathematics / John Williams &
  Nick Easingwood.
    p.   cm.
  1. Mathematics–Computer-assisted instruction.
  2. Mathematics–Study and teaching (Primary)–Data
  processing. 3. Educational technology. I Title: ICT and
  primary mathematics. II. Easingwood, Nick. III. Title.
  QA20.C65W55 2004
  372.7´044–dc22   2004000258

ISBN 0–415–36959–2

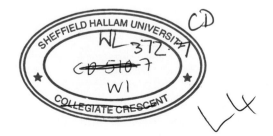

For Alastair, with love
1968–2003

Contents

List of illustrations

About the authors

John Williams has worked in Primary Education for over 30 years as Class Teacher, Head Teacher, Advisor for Science, Governor and as Senior Lecturer in Higher Education. It was during his time as a Head Teacher in Kent that he realised the potential of ICT in education, and his school was one of the first in the country to use computers for teaching primary age children. He has written over 20 classroom books on primary science and design and technology. He has recently retired from full-time teaching at Anglia Polytechnic University, where he was the Admissions Tutor and a lecturer responsible for the teaching of design and technology to student teachers. By dividing his time between Italy and the UK, he remains involved with primary education, lecturing, supervising students in schools, and of course more writing. His other interests include research into various aspects of the history of science.

Nick Easingwood is Senior Lecturer for ICT in Education and acts as the ICT Co-ordinator for the School of Education of Anglia Polytechnic University in Chelmsford, Essex. Apart from leading a Post-Graduate Certificate of Education (PGCE) Secondary ICT course, he also contributes to Primary and other Secondary Initial Teacher Education courses, as well as in-service Bachelors and Masters degree courses. He maintains regular contact with schools through visiting students on their school experiences, having himself spent 11 years as an Essex primary school teacher. His research interests include the development of online resources for student teachers and their capabilities in ICT on entering higher education. His publications include *ICT and Literacy* (2001), which he jointly edited, as well as a contribution to the second edition of *Beginning Teaching, Beginning Learning*, edited by Janet Moyles and Gill Robinson, published in April 2002. John and Nick have also jointly written *ICT and Primary Science*, which was published by RoutledgeFalmer in July 2003.

Foreword

There is a relationship between the human mind, the modern computer and mathematics which is often misunderstood. Indeed, over centuries, humankind has used the developing concept of the computer as a metaphor for the mind, and the growing knowledge of the human mind as a metaphor for the computer. It is now unclear which was the chicken or which the egg. This interchange of conceptions suggests a central place for the computer in our culture, that the often heard, but rather dismissive remark, 'it's just a tool', can underestimate.

It can be persuasively argued that tools and technology have been at the heart of intellectual endeavour since the Stone Age, and that the sciences and mathematics owe a debt to tools, rather than the reverse, as a source of intellectual development in our culture.

Since mathematical concepts and logic lie at the heart of the computer's function, it comes as no surprise that the study of mathematics and the use of ICT may be profitably intermingled. The concepts of algorithm, function, operation and set all have concrete manifestation in the world of computers to parallel their abstraction in mathematics. One consequence is that the computer, through the spreadsheet, database, LOGO programming, and modelling and simulation environments, has the delightful capacity to make concrete of the otherwise abstract ideas of relationship and process. For example the mathematical variable in algebra is often a mysterious object: 'Please miss, tell me how much x is?' The same (but subtly different) X on a computer, although capable of varying, can always be known as a value at any given time. A spreadsheet cell containing a function always shows an answer, for the moment. Suddenly, elusive mathematical ideas become tangible and may be played with, bringing dead algebra to a 'what if?' life. So far so good – it seems that there is already an impressive case for doing mathematics, practically, with a computer.

But in fact, there is even greater scope, because the computer has added to this capacity for logic and computation a unique facility to integrate and generate visual and dynamic material – multimedia – and to portray the most aesthetically pleasing visual and musical outputs based on mathematical data. Using LOGO and other software to discover geometry empowers us to pin down elusive abstractions with concrete experiences. LOGO also encourages us to benefit from our kinaesthetic, body-centred capacities when solving problems by acting 'turtles' ourselves.

In all of these ways, mathematics and the computer can combine to appeal to our multiple intelligences and raise the stakes for capability in learning mathematics.

But sadly, the potential identified here is often missing – why? – perhaps in part because such experiences have not been lived by many of today's teachers. Hence the purpose of this book: to begin to unlock the genie in the bottle and promote creativity in mathematics teaching and learning through practical advice and relevant detail.

Such advice is legion in this book, with valuable commentary to reassure the inexperienced teacher so that they may tackle both statutory and unspoken expectations, from the National Curriculum and the Numeracy and Literacy Strategies, with carefully explained and justified lesson ideas.

Pupils will also benefit from the appropriate deployment of ICT in mathematics advocated here: the handling of data and creation of graph and chart which may come from speedy ICT tools and the teacher's knowledge, enhanced by this book's exposition, coupled with the generation of their own data and purposes conspire to make the exploration of mathematical concepts both meaningful and relevant. Genuine 'what if?' questions may be asked and answered, alternatives judged and genuine inquiry fostered – the 'quantitative' improvement in the speed of production brought about by ICT begins to change the 'qualitative' nature of engagement with mathematics.

With the confidence that this book will inspire, the truth and beauty that excites successful mathematicians may begin to be appreciated by a much wider audience of teachers and learners, and the symbiotic relationship between our society and its most powerful tools may be continued, to all humankind's benefit.

Richard Millwood
Reader, Ultralab, Anglia Polytechnic University

Acknowledgements

The authors would like to thank the following companies, schools, organisations and individuals for their support and help in the writing of this book.

Suppliers

2Simple Software, 3–4 Sentinel Square, Brent Street, Hendon, London NW4 2EL
Commotion Group, Unit 11, Tannery Road, Tonbridge, Kent TN9 1RF
Data Harvest Group Limited, Woburn Lodge, Waterloo Road, Linslade, Leighton
     Buzzard, Bedfordshire LU7 7NR
Granada Learning Ltd (Black Cat), Granada Television, Quay Street, Manchester
     M60 9EA
Logotron Ltd, 124 Cambridge Science Park, Milton Road, Cambridge CB4 0ZS
Microsoft UK, Microsoft Campus, Thames Valley Park, Reading RG6 1WG
Promethean Ltd, TDS House, Lower Philips Road, Blackburn, Lancashire BB1 5TH
RMPLC, Unit 140 Milton Park, Abingdon, Oxon OX14 4SE
Valiant Technology, Valiant House, 3 Grange Mills, Weir Road, London
     SW12 0NE

Schools

The authors would particularly like to thank the staff and children of the following schools for the help, co-operation and hospitality shown to them during the writing of this book:
Letchmore Infants and Nursery School, Stevenage, Hertfordshire
Kenningtons Primary School, Aveley, Thurrock
St Nicholas CofE (VA) Primary School, Letchworth Garden City, Hertfordshire
Westbury Primary and Nursery School, Letchworth Garden City, Hertfordshire

Other thanks

Our thanks are extended to artist Liz Ballard for allowing us to use her artwork in Chapter 9.
Our thanks are also extended to colleagues from the School of Education of Anglia Polytechnic University, Chelmsford, Essex, with particular thanks to Mark Miller.

Illustrations

Screenshots reprinted by permission from Microsoft Corporation.
Microsoft is a trademark of the Microsoft Corporation
Line drawings Figures 1, 2, 3, 5.10, 5.11, 5.12, 5.13, 7.1, 8.1, 8.2, 8.3, 8.4, 8.5, 9.1, 9.2, 9.3, 9.4, 9.28, 10.1, 10.2, 10.3, 10.4, 10.6, 10.7, 10.8 by John Williams
Line drawings 9.10, 9.11, 9.12, 9.13, 9.14, 9.15, 9.16, 9.17, 9.18 by Liz Ballard
Illustrations 5.8, 5.9, 10.9, 10.10, 10.11, 10.12, 10.13,10.14 by John Williams and Nick Easingwood
Photographs 4.4, 4.5, 4.6, 4.7, 4.8, 4.9, 4.10, 4.11, 9.19 by Nick Easingwood
Photographs 9.6, 9.7, 9.8, 9.9 by Liz Ballard
Photographs 7.20, 7.22, 7.23, 7.24 by Westbury School, Letchworth Garden City, Hertfordshire
Photographs 8.9 and 8.10 by Letchmore Infants and Nursery School, Stevenage, Hertfordshire
All other illustrations by pupils of the schools detailed above

Figures from suppliers

2Simple (5.1, 5.2, 5.3)
Granada – Black Cat (1.1, 1.2, 1.3, 1.4, 1.5, 1.6, 1.7, 3.4, 3.5, 3.6, 7.3, 7.4, 7.5, 7.6, 7.7, 7.8, 7.9, 7.10, 7.11, 7.12, 7.13, 7.14, 7.15, 7.16, 7.17, 7.18, 7.19, 7.25, 7.26, 7.27, 7.28, 7.29, 8.6, 8.7)
Logotron (5.4, 5.5, 5.6, 5.7)
Data Harvest (8.8)
Microsoft (2.1, 2.2, 2.3, 3.3, 4.1, 4.2, 4.3, 5.8, 5.9, 6.1, 6.2, 6.3, 6.4, 6.5, 6.6, 6.7, 9.21, 9.22, 9.23, 9.24, 10.9, 10.10, 10.11, 10.12, 10.13,10.14)
Promethean (3.1, 3.2, 3.3, 3.7, 3.8, 3.9, 3.10, 3.11, 3.12, 3.13, 3.14, 3.15, 3.16, 3.17, 3.18, 3.19, 3.20, 9.5, 9.20, 9.25, 9.26, 9.27)
Research Machines – (8.11, 8.12, 8.13)
Valiant Technology (4.10, 4.11)

Why is it that it is considered socially acceptable to be 'not good at maths'? Few people would admit to being 'bad' at English, even when they are, although some will admit ruefully that they do not speak a foreign language. Of course we should be able to admit to our deficiencies – it is only in schools that we are meant to be good at everything – but many people seem to take an almost perverse pleasure in not knowing any mathematics at all.

There may be several reasons for all this. If the subject was badly taught, then we can blame the teaching. However, that would also apply to other subjects. Is it possible that there is a 'number blindness' similar to the 'word blindness' that hampers children's learning of English? A kind of mathematical dyslexia? There is research, both physiological and educational, that suggests this could be the case. The sooner this is both proven and recognised the better.

Even if these inherent difficulties are fully recognised, there remains the question of how best to teach the subject. Mathematics is perhaps the easiest subject to teach badly. It is not just that some people think that rote learning is still an essential component, or that pages of sums, all similar and all wrong or correct, depending on the children's basic understanding, may be required to show that 'work' has been done! Perhaps it is rather a lack of in-depth knowledge on the part of many teachers, coupled with a misunderstanding of the very nature of mathematics and why it is there at all.

We do not blame teachers, although we do ask them to think hard about their methods of teaching. We know that in today's world this is difficult. When there are SATS (Standard Assessment Tests) to be 'sat', with their and the schools' futures at stake, how else can children answer basic questions without some repetitive teaching and testing? Not too long ago the best primary schools offered the children some exciting maths. Vectors, co-ordinates and some very interesting geometry were part of their curriculum. They are not found so very often today, although perhaps they are being saved for the sixth form. Let us hope that the children can stay interested long enough!

Of course, what could be called the basic grammar of mathematics has to be known. Not having a basic understanding of the 'rules' of the subject must be akin to a footballer or a batsman at cricket attempting to play without knowing how to kick a ball or hold a bat. However, once these sportsmen learn the basic techniques they quickly go on to higher things. What boring games they would play if these basics were all they could or were allowed to do. In mathematics, therefore, primary school children do need to learn how to add, subtract, and eventually to multiply and divide. However, where possible they should also understand exactly what they are doing with the numbers during these processes, how to manipulate and handle numbers themselves, and whenever possible go beyond these basic techniques and learn about such things as graphs, shapes, sequences, and some of the early history of mathematics.

The present National Curriculum, and the ever-increasing emphasis on testing, makes this difficult. The fact that much of mathematics is very abstract may be obvious. However, this may not always be recognised in the classroom, or indeed the home. What does the young child make of a number – any number? What, for example, does the idea of 'three' mean to an infant in the nursery or reception class? It is just a word, until he or she is given three 'concrete' objects. When we are talking to people from another country, and have no knowledge of their language, and want to communicate a number, we count on our fingers or draw a picture. In the recent past, one of the strengths of the primary school was that teachers were able to use these techniques to make concrete many of these abstract ideas. Of course many still do, but with ever-increasing pressures, it is arguable that children now have less time to assimilate this essential understanding of numbers.

How then do children learn mathematics? How do they learn to add or subtract, or to tackle more advanced work? By practice, by rote? Some do, and some even might enjoy doing it that way. The authors both know children in their classes who have asked if they may learn 'their tables' by heart, and of course we have let them do so. However, we would argue that even at this elementary level, these children are in the minority, and we should want to do something better for the majority. No doubt there are some teachers who would question the very idea of teaching multiplication tables at all. However, for those who do teach them, the authors have found that the oft-tried method of asking children to write them down in longhand is as good as any.

Two lots of two add up to four.
Three lots of two add up to six.
Four lots of two add up to eight.
Etc. etc. etc.

We have often found that even Year 2 children enjoy this. It takes away the fear for those (like us) who have difficulty in learning by rote, and very importantly, children soon see the patterns emerging. They soon cotton on to the fact that all that multiplication amounts to is a quick way of adding. It may even be difficult to stop them! After six sheets of paper, the children may well have found that 240 lots of two add up 480. However, as they by then have a real understanding of what is going on, it is not a waste of time, or even paper.

There are many other mathematical activities that can only be done in a practical way. The Numeracy Hour itself suggests various methods. We have often met teachers who have recently returned from a National Numeracy Strategy 'Inset' (in-service training) course, and are very enthusiastic for the practical methods of teaching that they have learned. All to the good, although we do wonder what methods they were using before, as many of these 'new' methods were part of the everyday primary classroom several years ago! These practical methods at the most basic level are not just 'suitable' for primary age children, but are essential for an understanding of the wider aspects of the subject, and perhaps more important still, act as a motivation for further learning. Although the authors do not accept that learning should be an educational assault course, by the very nature of things, some areas of any subject may be more interesting to different children than are others, and therefore the curriculum should never be allowed to become too abstract and constricted. Hence we should include practical work such as the basics of symmetry. At any level of Key Stage 2, this can be simply illustrated by using a sheet of paper, a pencil and a pair of scissors (see Figure 0.1).

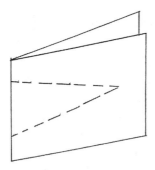 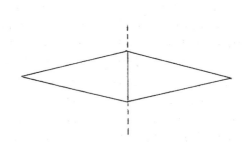

Figure 0.1 Fold a sheet of paper. Draw and cut any regular shape to show simple single axis symmetry.

There are numerous mathematical paper-and-scissor exercises that are suitable for children of this age, from simple nets drawn to construct solids, to helping children to understand about angles and shapes.

More paper-and-scissors mathematics

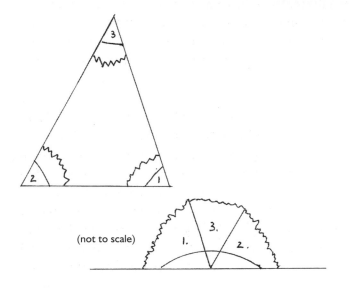

(not to scale)

Figure 0.2 Cut the corners off a triangle. Arrange them along a straight line to show 180 degrees.

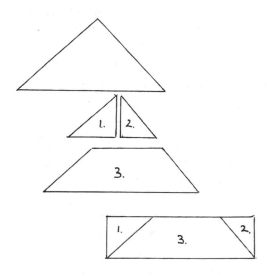

Figure 0.3 Finding the area of a triangle can be simpler if it is made into a rectangle.

Activities like those shown in Figures 0.2 and 0.3 can be found in various texts and curriculum materials if the teacher has enough time and energy to look. However, although they are in the National Curriculum, they do not seem to feature largely in most schools' numeracy hours, and therefore may not find their way into the classroom. The authors hope that this book will encourage the reader to use information and communication technology (ICT) as an aid to all areas of mathematics, and to allow the teacher and children to explore a wider range of activities. The few examples so far shown are all activities that lend themselves to the use of the computer. The multiplication tables can be done as a straightforward word-processing exercise, whilst any simple drawing program can be used for the shapes.

Of course there are many ready-made programs that the teacher can use. These will be discussed later in the book, along with how they can help children to better understand the relevant aspects of mathematics. This book is not intended to be a user's manual for computing, nor a mathematics textbook. Nevertheless, it will include many practical suggestions of how ICT can be used in the classroom, as well as giving various examples of the mathematics that children can experience. If some of the latter seem to be dangerously associated with the so-called 'New Maths' of the 1960s and 1970s, the authors offer no apologies. It was often a misunderstood term anyway, and much of the mathematics included in it is still being taught, albeit to older children. At the time, it was all carefully produced for primary children, and we well remember the fun the children had with it, as well as the ease with which they understood some really advanced ideas. (This may not have been the case at the time with some of us – teachers or parents.) Such work could be found in schemes such as The Kent Maths Project, or in books such as the 'Maths Adventure' series – not a title that would be used today. Where relevant, we have acknowledged these examples in the text, or in the bibliography found at the end of each chapter; however, much of the book is written from the authors' own experiences.

All this mathematics was being used in the classroom before the advent of the school-based computer, or at the very least during its early experimental stage. One of the authors well remembers his experiences with the early use of classroom computers in the early 1980s. The problem then was that there was very little in the way of good software, so that the computer had virtually to be used only as a word processor, although if you had the expertise it could produce simple block graphs and pie charts. However, by the mid-1980s some very good software was being developed. For example, DART, an early LOGO package for the BBC computer, was a simple yet very effective means of bringing a powerful new learning tool to the primary classroom in general, and to mathematics in particular. Indeed, as the technology steadily improved over the course of the next decade or so, the software to accompany it developed too. However, much of this software was designed to meet the demands of a rapidly expanding home market, and although some of the sound, graphics and video clips were impressive, the educational philosophy underlying them was not. As a result of this, and the corresponding introduction of the first National Curriculum, it appeared that much Mathematics and ICT teaching was actually more powerful and effective using a basic LOGO package in the mid-1980s than with more sophisticated software developed during the 1990s.

So at what stage of educational development are we now? We believe that the proper use of ICT (which, although primarily concerned with computers and associated software, also includes digital cameras and scanners), will allow the teacher to provide their children with a broader and more varied mathematics curriculum, despite the constraints of time, and the necessity to cover the requirements of the National Curriculum and the Numeracy Hour.

This can happen because a computer is a very powerful and flexible tool. It processes huge amounts of vastly different types of data and information simultaneously and at a rapid speed. It can be used for word processing, for handling data, producing presentations and publications, capturing images, creating pictures, acting as a means for sending and receiving e-mail and for accessing the Internet. Moreover, this can be done in an integrated way, so work produced in one application can be immediately cut and/or copied and pasted into another. Due to the provisional nature of this work it can be changed and saved as many times as is necessary, which means that it can be endlessly developed or edited, depending on the user's requirements. This power and flexibility that commerce and industry takes for granted is now widely available for primary school teachers and their pupils.

However, it should not be taken for granted that the power and flexibility of the computer is automatically exploited every time the hardware is switched on. The child needs to be placed firmly in control of the computer, interacting with it to help to develop mathematical knowledge, skills and understanding. It is therefore reliant on the teacher to establish a learning environment and a culture where this can actively happen. This will mean ensuring that the computer is used in such a way that it provides a 'value-added' component to teaching and learning, that it provides something that otherwise would not be available. For example, the graph-drawing facility of a range of data-handling applications enables the user to produce graphs and charts instantly once appropriate data have been entered into the computer. As the computer is acting as a labour-saving device, the children are removed from the time-consuming task of drawing a graph, enabling them to concentrate on the higher order skills of interpretation and analysis. This is not to say that the children should never draw graphs – indeed, as we explain later, drawing graphs is a very important skill, but there may be little value in the children producing the same types of graph every time that data-handling is covered. The time that was previously spent on this relatively low-level activity can be spent more valuably on the interpretation of the information itself. This will ensure that ICT is used to extend children's thinking and it will allow them to access levels of understanding that were previously unattainable.

As far as mathematics is concerned, there are many ways in which ICT can be used to enhance the teaching and learning experience. We have already described above one small example of a powerful use of ICT in this context, but there are many others that can be used. This book gives many examples of work that fall easily into the everyday experiences of the primary school child. These will include suitable programs to use for class topics involving databases, as well as some science topics, from which we will extract the important mathematics, and suggest how best the data can be displayed. We shall also discuss the general use and management of computers in the school, together with the value of other aspects of ICT such as the interactive whiteboard. There are also chapters on LOGO, and reference is made to various other ways in which other areas of mathematics can involve the use of the computer. It is not our intention to suggest that, by using ICT, the teacher should simply replace a page in a book for a page on a screen. We hope to show that ICT, used wisely, will enhance the teaching of mathematics, and help motivate and excite the child.

We trust that in this book we show that mathematics is not only an essential tool for the scientist and technologist, but is also a relevant and essential part of everyday life. We also hope that we have shown it to be an innately interesting intellectual pursuit in itself. These may not be terms readily associated with the primary classroom, particularly if the emphasis is only upon 'the basics'. If mathematics is taught only as a utilitarian subject, only useful when applied to other subjects, then children will be denied many exciting and challenging experiences.

In 1694, Sir Isaac Newton, who was of course both a scientist and a mathematician, was asked to comment on the mathematical curriculum then being taught at Christ's Hospital School. He objected to the teaching which he said was done 'by imitation, as a Parrot does so speak', and then went on to explain his objections:

A Vulgar Mechanick (sic) can practice what he has been taught or seen done, but if he is in an error he knows not how to find it out and correct it, and if you put him out of his road he is at a stand; Whereas he that is able to reason nimbly and judiciously about figure, force, and motion, is never at rest till he gets over every rub.

Bibliography

DfES/QCA, *The National Curriculum for England*, HMSO, London, 1999.
Dyscalculia, http://www.bbc.co.uk/skillswise/tutors/expertcolumn/dyscalculia/index.shtml (accessed 14 March 2004).
Gjertsen, D., *The Newton Handbook*, Routledge & Kegan Paul, London, 1986.
Monk, C., *Kent Mathematics Project*, Ward Lock Educational, London, 1979.
Stanfield, J. *et al.*, *Maths Adventure Series*, Evans, London, 1979.
Turnbull, H.W., Scott, J.F. and Hall, A.R. (eds), Newton, Sir Isaac, *The Correspondence of Isaac Newton*, 7 Volumes, Cambridge University Press, Cambridge, 1959–77.

Note

Although not an SI (International) Unit, centimetres are too convenient a measurement not to be used in the primary school, and therefore are used throughout this book.

Chapter 1

Planning the mathematics lesson

If you have read our companion volume, *ICT and Primary Science* (Williams and Easingwood, 2003), much of what follows will be familiar. We discuss these key issues again here purely because we believe that you cannot have a book about ICT and mathematics, or indeed ICT and any subject, and not include guidance as to how the lesson should be planned, organised, resourced, managed and delivered. If ICT is to be successfully incorporated into any lesson then these are fundamental issues that need to be tackled at a very early stage. The subsequent success of the lesson depends upon this. Employing ICT as part of a mathematics lesson is not difficult, but it adds another dimension and the place and purpose of it needs careful consideration. The introduction detailed *why* ICT should be used in the teaching of primary mathematics. This, and the following chapter, will expand upon this and detail *how* it can be used in terms of the practicalities that are involved, such as planning, organising, resourcing and managing the subject. It will also consider the actual teaching, and of course the outcome, i.e. how the children benefit and learn by using ICT.

The most important point to make about the use of ICT is that it cannot and should not replace the teacher. Excellent teaching and effective learning can only occur when a good teacher is present. The key lies in how the technology is used and employed, not in the teaching of the technology itself. As we saw in the Introduction, although computers have many assets, the ability to think for themselves, get to know each one of their pupils on a personal level, engage in conversation about their interests, plan, prepare and assess their work on an individual basis, or interact with their parents at open evenings, are not as yet within their capability. It is these things that make the teacher's role so crucial.

Planning the ICT lesson

So what does a mathematics lesson where ICT is to be used look like? Much of it will be reassuringly familiar, containing as it does all of the key features that one would expect in a plan for a primary mathematics lesson. This is detailed below:

- Selecting an appropriate topic: Why has a particular mathematics topic been chosen? Because it is in the National Curriculum for England, the National Numeracy Strategy or the Qualifications and Curriculum Authority (QCA) Schemes of Work? The idea for the work needs to have come from somewhere. It might even come from the teacher!

- Key learning objectives: What are the intended learning outcomes as a result of the lesson? What has informed the planning? These should be mathematics rather than ICT objectives. Although it may be possible to address several statements from the National Curriculum for ICT, these are secondary objectives. The primary ones must remain the mathematics objectives.

- Relevant connections and reference to the National Curriculum for Mathematics, the National Numeracy Strategy: It is maybe necessary to be able to directly connect to these, as this will ensure continuity and progression, and will illustrate how this particular lesson fits into an overall sequence.

- The content of the lesson: What exactly is to be taught?

- Details of any prior learning: The starting point may often be the children's previous experiences, and where this fits into the overall sequence mentioned above.

- Teaching methodology to be used: Particularly crucial whenever ICT is involved. Is the lesson to be a practical lesson where other equipment apart from the computer is to be used? Or will the entire lesson be computer-based?

- Key teaching points: What are you actually going to teach the pupils? What are you going to say to them? What are you going to ask them so as to ensure that they learn what you want them to learn?

- Differentiation: This is particularly difficult in this context, as the teacher has to consider different abilities in ICT as well as in mathematics. But how are you going to differentiate? By ability? By previous experiences? Are any of the pupils on individual education plans (IEPs)?

- The foci for assessment: How are you going to assess what you hope the children have learned? What do you think they will have learned? What are the intended learning outcomes? Were there any unintended learning outcomes?

- Cross-curricular links: Are there any clear and relevant connections to other areas of the curriculum? Avoid contrived links at all costs. (In a later chapter we discuss mathematics and other areas at some length. Although some of the subjects may be unusual, we trust that the connections will be genuine.)

■ Follow-up work: Where does this lesson fit into an overall sequence of work?

■ Resources: What hardware or software is to be used? Is the equipment appropriate to the age and ability of the pupils and the intended learning outcomes? This could include computers, scanners, cameras, printers as well as more subject-specific mathematical equipment such as scales or rulers, or perhaps other ICT-related equipment such as calculators. Software also needs to be considered at this stage.

The above should reassure teachers as these are elements of any good lesson and should be present regardless of whether ICT is being used or not. At first glance it might appear that ICT has a surprisingly low profile, but this should reinforce the idea that ICT is embedded within the subject, and does not dominate it. The role of ICT is mostly to act as a tool for children's learning through the ability to organise, display and analyse the collected data. At all times the children remain engaged in the key mathematical enquiry skills of calculating, hypothesising, predicting, observing, recording and analysing; therefore, these must have a high profile in the lesson plan. Additionally, the teacher needs to consider the teaching methods that are to be used, including the use of focused but open-ended questioning that extends pupils' thinking about mathematical knowledge, and extends their understanding of the subject. A good lesson is reliant upon interactive, imaginative and creative teaching. The truly effective lesson where ICT is used occurs when the teacher ensures that the key features of the computers, the ones that give it the 'value-added' component – speed, automatic function, provisionality and interactivity – are all harnessed to the full. This is entirely reliant upon the teacher, not the technology.

When planning a mathematics lesson that includes the use of ICT, the teacher needs to be clear about the role that ICT will take. The National Curriculum for England stresses the importance of using ICT to support teaching and learning for all subjects and mathematics is one of the subjects that can benefit the most from this support. However, the very existence of a National Curriculum document for ICT ensures that it has the status of a subject in its own right. Although this book is primarily concerned with how ICT can support the teaching of primary school mathematics, there are however many strong elements of the ICT National Curriculum that can be successfully and effectively delivered through the teaching of mathematics. At Key Stage 1 this includes entering and storing information (finding things out) and selecting and adding information for particular purposes, planning and giving instructions to make things happen (developing ideas and making things happen). At Key Stage 2 this knowledge and these skills are extended to include the preparation and interpretation of information for development, the creation, testing and refinement of sequences of instructions to make things happen and to monitor and respond to events. Additionally, at Key Stage 2, there is a requirement to use simulations and explore models for the investigation and evaluation of changing values and the identification of patterns and relationships. Specific mention is also made of the need to ask open-ended, *what if?* type of questions. All of these requirements can be easily addressed in a way that provides an appropriate context, yet taking a primarily mathematical focus.

It needs to be remembered at all times when planning a lesson that a computer is a hugely powerful and very expensive tool that needs to be used effectively. It is the distinctive 'value-added' component that it offers teaching and learning that makes the computer such an effective instrument. For example, data collected as a result of practical mathematics work can be sorted and displayed in a number of different ways at the click of a mouse button. Information might be displayed as a graph or as a chart, and several different versions of each can be produced depending on how the user wishes to sort, display and analyse the information. Drawing graphs by hand can take a whole lesson, but by using a computer the time saved can be spent by the children engaging in higher order skills such as the analysis and interpretation of the information that is displayed in front of them. The practical element of the lesson has not been replaced, but the power of the computer has been harnessed to enable pupils to access levels of understanding that would not otherwise be available to them. It is the teacher's responsibility to ensure that this power is harnessed, and this is discussed below.

Planning the mathematics lesson where ICT is to be included

Why choose this topic and these objectives?

The opportunity for primary teachers to choose the topic of the lesson and devise the content is now rare. Usually the main objectives for a lesson or sequence of lessons will have been taken from the schools' long- and medium-term plans. These in turn will have been prepared subject to the requirements of the respective Mathematics and ICT National Curricula as well as the National Numeracy strategy for the given age group. These are the factors that directly determine what will be taught, and they will normally be drawn directly from the National Numeracy Strategy (it needs to be remembered that, unlike the National Curriculum for England, the National Numeracy Strategy is a non-statutory document), although they may have been prepared by the schools' mathematics co-ordinator. Wherever the planning originated it identifies what needs to be taught, and the way in which it could be taught. In this particular instance, though, we are principally interested in the objectives. As mentioned elsewhere in this chapter, these main objectives will have a definite mathematical, rather than ICT, focus and this component will be refered to in the relevant attainment targets from the National Curriculum Mathematics and National Numeracy Strategy documents.

Prior learning

As mentioned above, all lessons have to be informed by something, regardless of the source. Failure to make reference to a medium-term plan, scheme of work or the National Numeracy Strategy can lead to a lack of continuity and progression, whereby skills, knowledge and understanding are either omitted from year group to year group, or are repeated in different years without any progression on the part of the teacher or the learners. This was one of the problems recognised by those who advocated a National Curriculum in the first place and rightly highlighted this. Much good imaginative teaching did take place in many schools, but all too often it was never followed up as the children became older. Very often it was even ignored by the secondary school, and children found themselves – to use a mathematical metaphor – back at square one. It was inevitable that some kind of plan should be produced to correct this. The problem now is that we might have too many plans, and those that we have might be too inflexible. Nevertheless, the teacher needs to ensure that there is a structured progression, so that concepts, skills, knowledge and understanding are consistently taught through introduction, development and extension.

Teaching methodology

The teacher needs to consider how the lesson is to be taught, and this in turn will directly influence the section below, which concerns actual classroom techniques. These will depend largely on the content of the lesson, but the teacher may also want to make the lesson a practical one. The teacher will therefore need to devise activities that enable the children to engage in practical work and then enter the findings into the computer for subsequent analysis. Where possible, the teacher should base the methodology on relevant underlying educational theory. So, for example, if the teacher is delivering a lesson where LOGO is to be used, consideration needs to be given to the underlying philosophy as espoused by Seymour Papert, who in turn was strongly influenced by the writings of Jean Piaget. If the teacher appreciates exactly what it was that Papert was intending to do when developing the LOGO language, then the teaching strategies involved will be geared to facilitating experiential learning, rather than just directly instructing the children. This will involve providing appropriate resources and using a teaching style that employs open-ended questioning and a considered approach that allows the children to learn through 'doing'. It would be wholly inappropriate for pupils to be sitting at a computer and being told what to type into a LOGO program in 'battery hen' mode.

Teaching points

If the previous section discussed the importance of methodology, then this section details what the teacher needs to say or do to ensure that the intended learning takes place. This is the 'nuts and bolts' section, where the teacher does most of the actual teaching.

Differentiation

This is a particularly difficult area because differentiation needs to refer to both the mathematics and the ICT. It is therefore especially important to consider it at the planning stage. In a typical primary school class, it is entirely possible that there may be pupils who are high attainers in mathematics but lower attainers in ICT. Indeed, there may be up to seven years mathematical ability span in any typical Key Stage 2 class (DES, 1982). Conversely, high-attaining ICT users may struggle with mathematical concepts. Given that the focus of the lesson remains solely on the mathematics component, with the power of the computer being engaged to develop the appropriate mathematical knowledge, skills and understanding, then this apparent contradiction should actually assist the teacher in solving the potential difficulty. The teacher can harness the children's abilities in one area to help those with difficulties in another. The issue of differentiation highlights clearly the point at which the skill and professional judgement of the teacher becomes crucial and helps to explain why the teacher can never be replaced by a computer.

Despite the main focus of the lesson being firmly upon the mathematics, it remains important that the ICT being used is appropriate to the capabilities of the pupils and to the teaching and learning objectives for that particular lesson. There is always a danger that it will be incorrectly matched to ability. This may be due to the teacher's general lack of experience in the use of ICT within the lesson or because the teacher has a particular knowledge of a piece of software that he or she knows will work, and thus tries to use it in the wrong context. An example of this might be in choosing to use a Key Stage 2 piece of software for Key Stage 1 or vice versa, even though the mathematical concepts to be taught are relevant and appropriate.

Assessment

Crompton and Mann (1997) have stated the main problem with assessment where ICT is involved is that many teachers see the word 'technology' and misinterpret exactly what this means, electing to assess the child's use of the computer, rather than the subject element that should provide the main focus for this. Therefore, it is extremely important to determine how assessment is to be undertaken at the planning stage, as it forms an integral part of the planning–assessment–planning cycle. It should be recognised that a child's progress may have been hampered simply by an inability to enter information, perhaps due to unfamiliarity with the keyboard or the program, and therefore the focus of the assessment must remain on the mathematics content. As a consequence of this, assessment is not an afterthought to the lesson; it is an integral part of it and is used for the following reasons:

- To determine whether teaching has been effective. Have the children learned what you intended them to learn? Were there any unintended outcomes? If so, are they relevant?
- Were all of the intended learning outcomes covered?
- Were the children working at an appropriate level?
- What additional practice may they need?
- Which concepts, knowledge and skills need to be reinforced? Which ones need to be extended?
- Where next do the children need to go with this topic?

Effective planning for children of differing ability levels can only occur when the teacher is aware of the level at which the children are working. If a task is too easy or too difficult then learning will not take place. This will usually be determined through the use of formative assessment, which in turn informs future planning. The teacher will determine what other criteria are needed to indicate whether or not progress has in fact been made. Although summative and diagnostic assessments will occasionally need to be used, the largely practical and investigative nature of ICT and mathematics will dictate that in the main, formative assessment methods are necessary. These will include determining whether any problem-solving techniques were used, and if so which ones, how long the children remained on task, and the levels of collaborative discussion by the pupils.

Cross-curricular links

Although it can be argued that both the National Curriculum for Mathematics and the National Numeracy Strategy do not readily appreciate or identify links to other areas of the curriculum, the authors are committed to this very important aspect of primary education. Any such links need to be identified at the planning stage. Mathematics is a subject that at the primary stage at least should be mainly practical in nature. Even for non-mathematicians it is an essential part of everyday life. Whether it is calculating the change for an article purchased in a shop, measuring up a house for curtains or carpets, weighing out ingredients for cooking, or even something as relatively straightforward as finding a direction, practical mathematics plays a fundamental part in the process. Yet both the National Curriculum and the National Numeracy Strategy appear not to recognise that it is not only a question of being able to 'do' maths, but that, most fundamentally of all, if mathematics teaching is to have both meaning and value, it needs to be applied into a wide range of contexts that may include other subjects. This would particularly involve science, where data handling directly relates to both subjects.

Quite apart from the need to place mathematics into a practical context, there is the need to recognise that today's high-tech, primary-school child actually does learn in an integrated manner. Constant exposure to a wide range of integrated visual and audio media such as television, video, DVD, mobile telephones, multimedia applications, e-mail and the Internet ensures children do not learn isolated skills or pieces of knowledge in a manner which is divorced from either other subjects or the world around them. A cross-curricula approach also offers the teacher the only opportunity to cover all of the requirements of the various National Curriculum documents and national strategies in any degree of depth.

What does the teacher need to consider?

The most fundamental question to ask at the planning stage is whether the use of ICT is appropriate in order to achieve the teaching and learning objectives of the given lesson. When making this decision, the teacher needs to consider whether there will be a 'value-added' component: that is, will there be any clear gains to teaching and learning? Will the use of ICT improve the teacher's teaching and will it enhance the learning experience for the children? Once we have assumed that both aspects will be satisfactory, then planning for the lesson can begin. In the context of this chapter, we are assuming that it is appropriate to use ICT to support the mathematics lesson. Therefore, working from the starting point that ICT is to be used, the teacher then needs to consider her or his resources.

Resources

Although a cliché, the phrase 'Fail to prepare, prepare to fail' is a useful rule of thumb when planning and delivering any lesson, but especially when there is a strong practical element involved. All lessons need to be resourced to a certain extent and this needs to be made explicit on the lesson plan. Careful consideration needs to be given to this, as these are the tools by which the lesson will be delivered. These must be prepared and made ready prior to the start of the lesson. Failure to do so can lead to the teacher feeling underprepared and thus lacking in confidence. If key equipment needed for the lesson is missing, then effective and efficient teaching may be prevented altogether. If computers are not switched on or logged on, or printers do not have any ink in them, or the batteries for the digital camera are flat, then any of these will prevent the intended teaching objectives from taking place and thus will delay the progress of the lesson. This could be very significant if the lesson is taking place in a heavily timetabled ICT suite. It is of course important to ensure that the resources that are selected are appropriate to the lesson's objectives.

Hardware

As far as mathematics and ICT are concerned, the required resources could be quite extensive. They might involve the use of mathematical apparatus such as metre sticks, trundle wheels, compasses, tape measures, books, charts or posters, as well as generic equipment for working outside of the classroom such as clipboards, worksheets, pencils and paper. For the ICT component this could be much more extensive. These might include:

- Computers: These might be the more 'traditional' desktop computers in a classroom or ICT suite, or perhaps even laptops that can be used outside of the traditional learning setting. If they have wireless networking, they can be used 'in the field' and still have network access for the Internet and e-mail, or for file sharing such as printing or allowing access to another group's files;
- Digital still and video cameras: These can be used for recording practical investigations. The images can then be shared with other users, or can be stored on the camera's chip for later use when writing up and/or presenting their investigation. The resulting images or video clips can be subsequently edited for use in a variety of ways, perhaps in a word document or a *Microsoft PowerPoint* presentation.
- Scanners: These are devices that act in a similar way to a colour photocopier, and enable the user to scan paper documents or images into the computer, which, like images from a digital camera, can then be used in a number of ways in the presentation of mathematical investigations.

Software

Arguably the most important resource in any lesson where ICT is used is the software. This is because software acts as the interface between the user and the computer, and is the means whereby the power of the computer is harnessed. We have already mentioned that the computer has the power to handle large amounts of a wide range of data types, quickly, automatically and interactively through its ability to sort, search, interrogate, analyse, and subsequently display the final data. It is the wide range of software such as word processors, desktop publishing packages, spreadsheets, graphics packages, e-mail and Internet browsers that enable the user to take advantage of these principal features.

For their part the users interact with the software to bring creativity and original thought to the learning situation. The creativity and ideas that the user possesses will contribute to the choice of the software that will allow the computer to function interactively. The quality of the learning will be largely determined by the quality of the software and how it is used. When selecting software the teacher needs to consider its relevance to the mathematics being taught and the age and ability of the children who will use it. After all, the better the software, the better the lesson and the better the learning.

What makes good educational software?

Any software that is used must be appropriate for meeting the objectives of the lesson, the chosen activity and the tasks that will be given to the children. It should have the necessary flexibility and be sufficiently interactive to make it easy enough for the children to use and it should accurately match the requirements of what a good lesson should contain, which we detailed at the beginning of this chapter. The software must fit into the teacher's preferred teaching style and use an appropriate model. If a teacher employs a teaching style that encourages group work and collaborative learning then she/he will obviously need to set up situations where the children can learn collaboratively. Therefore the software will need to be able to support this. This will mean employing generic or open-ended software which allows the children to use the computer as a tool to further their own learning by putting them in control of both computer and software, rather than using software which basically tells them what to do and requires a closed response, such as the simple answer to a sum. However, the teacher may wish to adapt her or his own style to fit in with the requirements and the structure of the program. This approach can become an example of how ICT can develop an individual teacher's knowledge, as well as allow both teacher and children to work beyond the narrow confines of a 'set' lesson.

The other key questions that a teacher needs to ask when selecting appropriate software to support the mathematics lesson are:

- Does the software teach the children what the teacher wants them to learn? Does it enhance the learning experience? Does it enable the teaching and learning objectives of the lesson to be met? This is of course fundamental, but is easily overlooked. There is little point in selecting software that does not do this.

- Is the software easy to use? Is it intuitive? In other words, can the children learn how to use the software efficiently with a minimum of teacher input? A teacher's principal job is to teach, not act as an ICT technician, so valuable lesson time needs to be spent on teaching the subject, not providing technical support. If there is a manual accompanying the software, it should be short and pitched at a level that the children can understand for themselves. If the manual is too long or too hard to understand, then the software may be too difficult to use and may therefore be inappropriate for that lesson. Any online or on-screen help should be short, helpful and easy to read. The whole point of using ICT is that it enhances the learning experience, not hinders it.

- Is the screen clear and easy to follow? Is it bright, attractive and appealing to the user? Children will be more readily engaged if this is the case.

- Can the icons be clicked easily? They should be large enough for younger users, and should use commands that are common to other pieces of software to support ease of use.

- Is the reading level appropriate to the reading age of the user? The text should not be too hard, or too easy. The pupil should be able to easily read any text for meaning.

- Is the content accurate and free of bias? This is particularly important whenever web sites are used, as there is little editorial control over material placed on the Internet. This can also apply to CD-ROMs where the author or publisher may have some kind of vested interest. There may be cultural differences or there may be a different perspective from our own on world events or people and places.

- Is there an option facility so that the teacher can change the ability level? The more flexible software allows this to happen, such as the *Black Cat Toolbox* from Granada, which allows children from both primary age key stages to access the same software, thus cutting down on purchasing costs and time in teaching the pupils how to use the package.

- Can the teacher change the difficulty level of the language? The teacher might even need to change the language itself if English is not the pupils' mother tongue.

- If the software is American, can it be converted from American English to UK English? If not, the teacher will have to make the children aware of differences between the two.
- Is a trial copy of the software available either as a download from a company web site or on approval through the post? It is always useful to have a look at the software first. It is unlikely that a school would purchase a series of mathematics textbooks without looking at them first, so why not apply the same criteria to software?
- Is the software compatible with the make and model of both computer and operating system? If the school's computers use the Windows XP operating system, can the software run on this platform? If it uses iMacs, is compatible software available?
- Can the software run quickly and smoothly on the computer and over the network? Do graphics, images and video clips display properly? (A program such as *Quick Time* may be needed.) Are suitable sound cards fitted, enabling the sound to work properly, and play back as it should, without any pauses for buffering? (This occurs when loading images and sound into the computer's memory.)
- Is there the opportunity to evaluate the software before purchase? Where possible, the teacher should always take the opportunity to evaluate the software using the criteria listed above, in exactly the same way that they would with any other educational medium before committing scarce financial resources. Most software publishers make their products available on approval, either as samples through downloads from their web sites or through the post for a trial period, usually for 30 days. However, these are often not the full versions of the programs, or they are 'timed out' in that they stop working once the end of the trial period has been reached. Many of the best publishers' web sites can be found at www.teacherxpress.com (note the spelling).

What is the place and purpose of software in the curriculum?

When planning the lesson the teacher has to decide how the software is to be used, particularly in relation to the way that the lesson is going to be organised and managed. This means that a decision needs to be taken on whether the software is to be used with the whole class, groups, pairs or individuals. Some software packages naturally lend themselves to one particular approach rather than another. For example, a drill and practice program will be more suitable for individual use, where a particular skill needs to be reinforced, whereas a data handling package such as a spreadsheet or database will encourage pairs or small group work. Whatever the context, the teacher needs to ensure that both organisationally and educationally, due regard is given to the type of software that is employed and, in particular, the way that it is used.

Generally speaking, there are four principal types of educational software. These are:
- Drill and Practice programs (where the computer is in control of the user)
- Revelatory Programs
- Conjectural or emancipatory programs
- Open-ended software (where the user is in control of the computer).

(After Kemmis, Atkin and Wright, 1977)

Drill and practice software

Following an objectives-based model of learning, this type of software is concerned with a teaching, or didactic, approach and usually takes the form of a series of structured questions and answers with the learner being very strongly led by the computer. The user answers a closed question that can only have one correct answer and the software responds accordingly. If the answer given is correct then the software will provide positive feedback and will move the user to the next level. However, if the answer is incorrect then the program will provide further practice and reinforcement at this level until the child can demonstrate competence. Generally speaking we would not recommend widespread use of this type of software, as it does not begin to harness the power and versatility of the modern computer. However, where an individual needs some reinforcement of a particular skill or concept, then this type of software can be useful. The computer, unlike the teacher or the child, does not become bored or frustrated, and can repeat the same question or types of questions any number of times, without any additional bias. This may be particularly useful for those children who are on individual education plans (IEPs). A more sophisticated development of this kind of software is the individual learning system (ILS), which is discussed elsewhere in this book.

Revelatory software

Although similar in many respects to the drill and practice software described above, revelatory software is geared more towards a learning, rather than a teaching, approach and usually involves educational or adventure games and simulations, which are usually CD-ROM or Internet based. An excellent example of this is the program *The Logical Journey of the Zoombinis*, which, as the name suggests is a program that is designed to extend children's logical mathematical thinking. Although still a very closed environment that is highly structured and objectives-based, the user has an increased input as there is a requirement to engage in decision making in order to proceed through the program. The user will usually be presented with several options of which one has to be selected in order to progress. This may involve simulations of real situations that can be modelled through the varying of external conditions, and can simulate a range of mathematical operations.

Conjectural

Sometimes referred to as the emancipatory category, this is where the computer is being used as a tool for learning by providing a framework within which the children can work. Here generic and common application software is used to act as tools in order to extend the way that children learn primary mathematics, and includes the use of databases, spreadsheets and graphics packages. In the mathematical context this enables the child to sort, search, retrieve and graph information, or write up and present their findings, discover patterns in sets of data, draw conclusions and engage in the higher-order thinking skills that ensures that the computer is being used in an appropriate, value-added way.

Open-ended software

This type of software puts the user firmly in control of the computer, rather than the other way round that typifies 'drill and practice' software. In the open-ended context the computer is being entirely controlled by the learner, where to all intents and purposes the child is engaging in programming. As far as primary mathematics is concerned, this would most obviously include programming through the use of screen and floor turtles in LOGO, where the child inputs commands and the turtle responds accordingly. Of course, to a certain extent there can never be a truly open-ended use, or even open-ended software, as all hardware or software has some limitations and constraints built into it by the designer and the programmer. However, the concept that children can be in complete control of the computer certainly exists and should be aimed for at all times.

Whatever software is used, it must be remembered, when determining the success of a lesson which involves the use of ICT, that nothing can replace high quality teaching. The software that is used may be the most appropriate and be the best available for a given task or activity, but if it is used inappropriately then the lesson cannot be successful. In order to assure this success, when using ICT, the teacher must first get to know the program thoroughly, so that all of the functions can be fully exploited and then directly applied to the subject content of the lesson that is being taught. In order to do this the teacher must ensure that the same rigour is taken when selecting software that would be taken with non-ICT resources. As we have already stated, the teacher must ensure that the chosen software does exactly what the intended learning outcomes demand. The use of poor or inappropriate software can seriously affect the quality of the lesson, while in the hands of a skilled teacher the use of the most appropriate software can provide excellent learning experiences.

Nevertheless, no matter how good the software, or even the quality of the teaching, actual practical mathematics should not be replaced by using ICT simply because it is there and available. The opportunity for children to handle mathematical equipment such as tape measures or trundle wheels is a vital component of the primary mathematics lesson. The most powerful use of ICT occurs when these practical activities are supported by the use of application software such as databases and spreadsheets. We have described in the Introduction to this book how the computer should to be used as a tool to extend children's mathematical learning through its ability to handle a wide range of different types of data quickly and interactively, much of which should be collected as raw data away from the computer.

Nevertheless, taking this idea one step further, when the child is put in complete control of the computer, for example when using LOGO, ICT becomes the key vehicle for the mathematics investigation itself. Other forms of ICT can then be used to present the findings. A digital camera may record the children programming, and this can then be inserted into a word-processing document as part of a *PowerPoint* presentation, so that the actual program commands that the children have typed can then be exported.

A long-term database case study – one school's approach to the long-term planning of mathematics and ICT

Our thanks to Bob Hopcraft, the Headteacher and ICT Co-ordinator of St Nicholas CofE (VA) Primary School, Letchworth Garden City, Hertfordshire, for this case study. Our thanks also to the Year 3 teacher and Mathematics Co-ordinator, Kate Page.

The unit described in this case study is designed to introduce children to larger relational databases, and the idea that large amounts of data can be handled efficiently and accurately by using a computerised database. The unit is part of the Spring Term ICT and Numeracy programme, and the children work at it for two sessions each week, using the RM *Information Workshop* program.

The work builds upon previous studies completed in Year 1, where the children use ICT to record traffic surveys that are conducted on the busy road outside the school. Year 3 children are therefore familiar with the idea of entering numerical information into a computer and analysing the subsequent graphical data. It also develops and extends their work in Mathematics relating to handling data, where they investigate problems by organising and interpreting numerical information, using simple lists, tables, and graphs. When they use the *Information Workshop* databases, the children need to call upon these skills, to use and develop them so as to enable them to interpret data and frame relevant questions relating to it.

Working with databases

The first sessions of the unit are paper-based and follow the teaching activities described in the Year 3 QCA Unit 3C 'Introduction to Databases'. Here children begin to realise the difficulties of handling and classifying large amounts of paper-based data. The children in this study had particular fun with newspapers when they were asked to find obscure stories from random pages. At this stage the children were introduced to using record cards, and using the information on them to draw and produce relevant graphs.

The children were then asked to make a set of up to six of these cards for the topic 'minibeasts'. They were introduced to the meaning of the terms 'record' and 'field', and there was much discussion about the need for accuracy in presentation and spelling.

When this part of the unit was completed the remainder of the time was spent in the school's ICT suite, where the children were shown how to enter their own information onto a database. Using *Information Magic*, part of the *Information Workshop* suite from *Black Cat*, they built their six record cards into a dataset entitled 'minibeasts'. Whenever possible the information for these cards came from a practical science topic previously carried out by the children. These are illustrated in Figures 1.1 and 1.2.

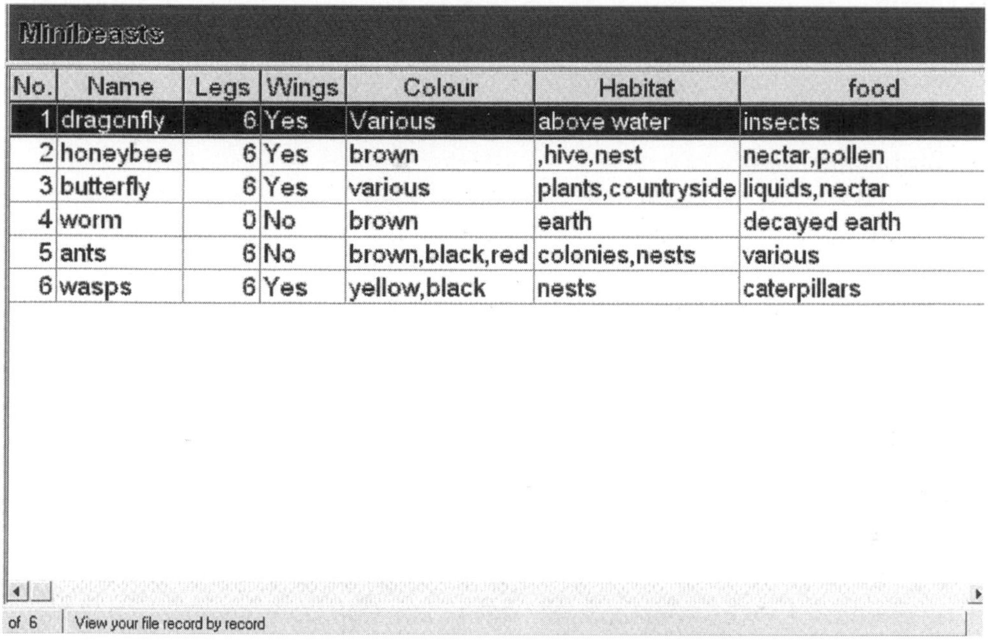

No.	Name	Legs	Wings	Colour	Habitat	food
1	dragonfly	6	Yes	Various	above water	insects
2	honeybee	6	Yes	brown	,hive,nest	nectar,pollen
3	butterfly	6	Yes	various	plants,countryside	liquids,nectar
4	worm	0	No	brown	earth	decayed earth
5	ants	6	No	brown,black,red	colonies,nests	various
6	wasps	6	Yes	yellow,black	nests	caterpillars

of 6 | View your file record by record

Figure 1.1 A child's database on the theme of 'minibeasts', using *Information Magic*.

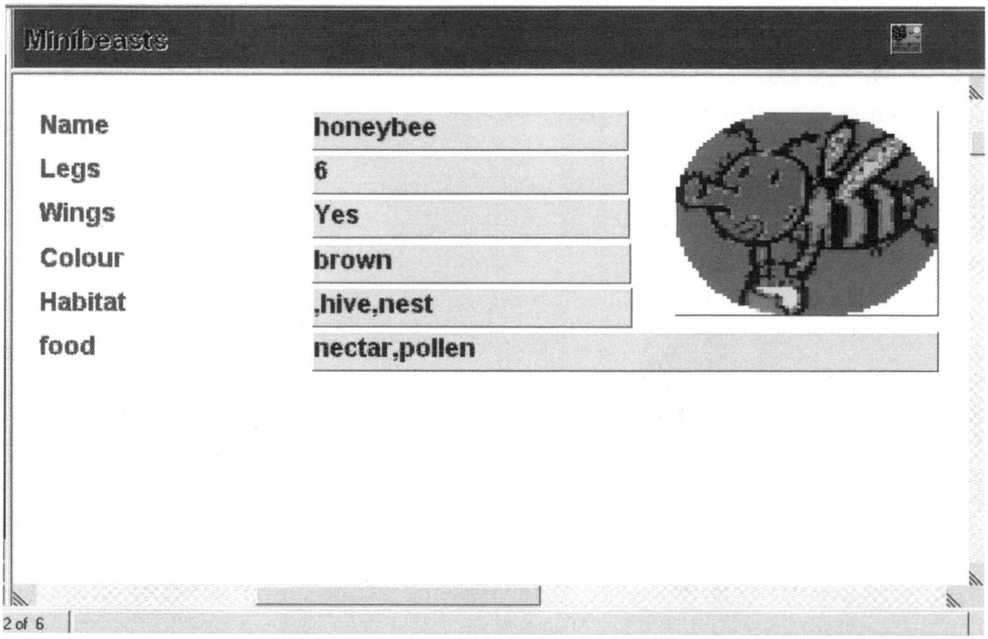

Minibeasts	
Name	honeybee
Legs	6
Wings	Yes
Colour	brown
Habitat	,hive,nest
food	nectar,pollen

2 of 6

Figure 1.2 Record number 2 of the 'minibeasts database', showing information for the honeybee, complete with imported image.

The children are then introduced to 'British birds', a pre-structured database that comes with the *Information Workshop* package. It holds 43 existing records, each supporting the following fields:

Bird name
Habitat
Food type
Size
Measure
Behaviour
Nest
Beak type
Colour
Flight pattern
Resident/migrant.

Of these fields, four are alphanumeric, one is numeric, and the remaining six have information entered from a multiple choice menu. Whilst children may add to or edit this database, the school tends to use it to encourage the children to analyse and interrogate the database. They are encouraged to sort the birds in various ways, such as grouping them into those that migrate or those that stay at home. They may sort them by size, or alphabetical order. Children explore the individual records and sets of records in the spreadsheet view. They are quickly able to draw graphs to help sort data. Three examples of simple sorts that are illustrated by a range of graphs are illustrated by Figures 1.3, 1.4 and 1.5.

Size

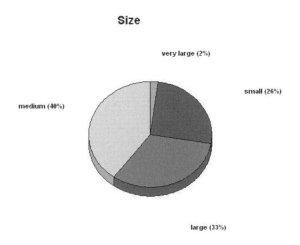

very large (2%)

small (26%)

medium (40%)

large (33%)

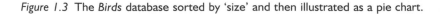

Figure 1.3 The *Birds* database sorted by 'size' and then illustrated as a pie chart.

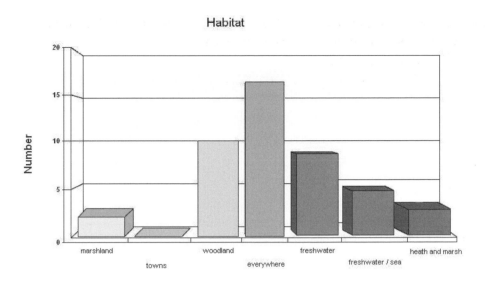

Figure 1.4 The *Birds* database sorted by 'habitat' and then illustrated as a bar chart.

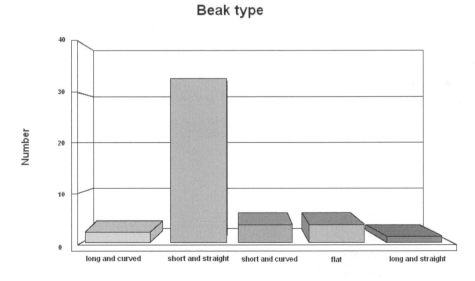

Figure 1.5 Different types of beak illustrated by a bar chart.

This can then be further extended by searching the 'beak types' to find those birds that have 'long and curved' beaks (Figures 1.6 and 1.7).

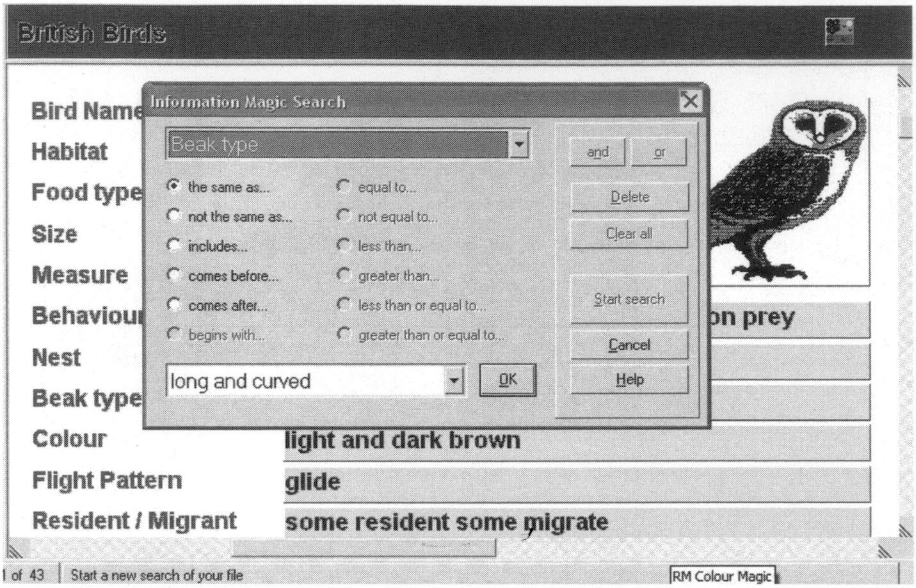

Figure 1.6 Example of a search by 'Beak type', the same as 'long and curved'. The listed results are illustrated by Figure 1.7.

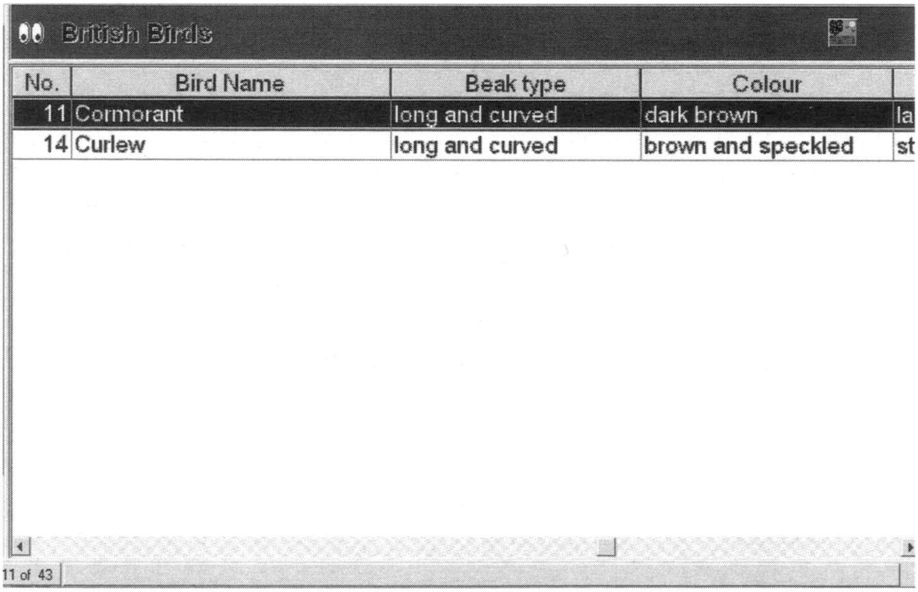

Figure 1.7 Record number 11, the cormorant, and record number 14, the curlew, have long and curved beaks.

The first time that the school tried this unit, the staff were surprised at the level of sophistication that could be so quickly attained by most of the pupils. However, some pupils that did find it more difficult and they were paired with more able children who were able to offer advice and support.

The children very quickly realised that the most important skill in using the database was being able to ask the right kind of question in the right way, and ensuring that their queries were reasonable and appropriate. They soon learned to use the accepted database jargon, using the necessary markers in order to find which birds fitted which categories. The class teacher produced worksheet questionnaires to help with this. Some of the children completed these by hand, but others were able to multitask and complete them on the screen. Finally, the children learnt to use the 'includes' command. They were then able to explore the more complex fields, for they had quickly realised the shortcomings of the simple 'is the same as' indicator.

Conclusion

The main purpose of this chapter is to emphasise the point that planning a mathematics lesson where ICT should be used is very similar to the planning of every other good lesson, although it does pose extra challenges (*not* problems) for the teacher. Regardless of the place and role of ICT, primary mathematics must remain a practical, hands-on subject that employs the key skills of calculating, hypothesising, predicting, analysing, observing, recording and drawing conclusions that are valid, reliable and meaningful. In order to do this it is important that collaborative learning and interactive teaching is employed. We have already stressed the importance of making sure that children do not become isolated and passive recipients of the material on the screen, in that they should interact with the computer as much as with their peers. For by using it in a context that demands composition, interrogation, analysis and the drawing of meaningful conclusions, rather than requiring simple yes or no answers or the memorisation of simple, isolated mathematical facts, real learning can take place. This is discussed in greater depth in the next chapter.

Bibliography

Briggs, M. and Pritchard, A., *Using ICT in Primary Mathematics Teaching*, Learning Matters, Exeter, 2002.

Crompton, R. and Mann, P. (eds), *IT Across the Primary Curriculum*, Cassell, London, 1997.

DES, *Mathematics Counts* (The Cockcroft Report), HMSO, London, 1982.

DfEE/QCA, *The National Curriculum for England*, HMSO, London, 1999.

Kemmis, S., Atkin, R. and Wright, E., *How do Students Learn? Working Papers on Computer Assisted Learning*, Centre for Applied Research in Education, University of East Anglia, Norwich, 1977.

Squires, D. and MacDougall, A., *Choosing and Using Educational Software: A Teachers' Guide*, The Falmer Press, London, 1994.

Chapter 2

Delivering the lesson

Once the plan has been written, the next step is the delivery of the lesson itself. The previous chapter discussed how lessons should be planned and what they should contain; this chapter will focus upon the key organisational and management issues concerning the teaching of a mathematics lesson where ICT is used. Although these aspects should be considered at the planning stage, we have dealt with them separately here for the sake of clarity. Structured and well-paced delivery of lessons is fundamental to all good teaching, and although this is specifically mentioned in the National Strategy documents, it can easily be overlooked as the teacher attempts to manage all of the required elements of the lesson.

The purpose of the lesson

From the outset the purpose of the lesson needs to be carefully considered. Although by no means mutually exclusive, there will be three main purposes:

■ To introduce a new concept or idea. This lesson might be the first in a sequence of lessons, or might be a key lesson further into that sequence, where a concept or idea needs to be explained again or extended. In either case the teacher will probably need to begin the lesson with an input session to describe what the new idea is, then give the children the opportunity to practise this for themselves. The lesson will conclude with a discussion of the new idea that has been learnt.

■ To reinforce an existing idea or concept. This will involve practising a particular skill, either through the use of practical activities or through more abstract text-book or CD-based work to apply theoretical ideas into a meaningful context.

■ To extend an existing idea or concept. In many respects this will be very similar to the first point above. Almost by definition, if a new concept or idea is being extended then new material is being covered.

The purpose of the lesson will directly influence how the teaching and the children's learning in the lesson will be organised, and will either take one of five distinct approaches, or may have elements of each during the course of a single lesson:

■ Where the children's main role will be as 'recipient' learners. This is currently the most common teaching and learning approach in primary schools, where the teacher introduces a concept or idea, or demonstrates a skill, which the children subsequently acquire and reinforce. This may occur when the teacher introduces a new mathematics topic or a new piece of software with which to develop their investigations (or both). The structure of a lesson such as this applies particularly closely to the three-part lesson described in the next section.

■ Where the children's main role will be as 'investigative' learners. This is where the children complete an activity where they are finding something out. This can be used on an individual, pairs or group basis and works particularly well in a collaborative learning context.

■ Where the children's main role is as peer tutors. This is where a group of pupils learn the key skill or concepts being taught and then 'tutor' the others. This is a particularly effective model where there may only be one or two computers in the classroom.

■ Where the children's main role is as collaborative learners. Collaborative learning occurs where children work together on a shared task to find a common outcome. The important point to remember is that the successful completion of the task is dependent on all members of the group, and is an educational rather than an organisational device. When using ICT this should ideally involve the children working in pairs, and should be employed even when there are enough computers for every member of the class or group being taught. This allows for pupil interaction and shared working on tasks. Pairs can be arranged in a number of ways including those of similar or differing abilities, different gender or even through different tasks. Groups of three or more should be avoided during the ICT element, as adult supervision will be needed to ensure that there is equal access to the keyboard and mouse, and equal effort from each member of the group.

■ Where the children are working individually. Occasionally, it will be necessary for individuals to work alone. This might be so that children can develop individual ideas or work individually on specific skills practice, perhaps using a CD-ROM or an Individual Learning System.

The teacher needs to ensure that the organisation is appropriate to the content of the lesson, is suitable for the age and ability of the children, and that an appropriate teaching style is being employed. For example, it would not be appropriate to give the children an activity that demands a practical approach, but then teach the whole lesson didactically, or not allow the children the opportunity to participate in collaborative and investigative learning. The children would be denied the rich learning experiences that this approach offers.

The structure of the lesson

Whatever the purpose of the lesson, it will normally take the form of a three-part lesson. This should involve:

- An introduction. This is where the key concept or skill being taught is introduced to the children.
- The practical section of the lesson. This is where the children engage in 'hands-on' activities to learn and reinforce the new material that is being taught.
- The plenary, where the new material is discussed. This should not be a simple question-and-answer session, or even where the children 'show and tell' what they have done in the lesson, but should reinforce and extend the children's learning through the use of sharply-focussed and open-ended key questioning.

At the beginning of the lesson the teacher should share the learning objectives with the children, and should explain why this particular lesson is being taught. We are all more motivated to complete a task when we can see a point to it. These objectives should be clear, challenging and based upon the results of previous learning. It is also important at this point to make explicit to the children that there are high expectations in terms of both behaviour and effort. This in turn will give pace to the lesson, and will ensure that all participants remain focussed and on task throughout. It is important to maximise the limited time of a lesson, especially if specialist equipment such as ICT equipment is involved.

All members of the class should be encouraged to participate from the outset. This is a particularly important point and is one that should not be underestimated. Both mathematics and ICT have often been perceived as 'boys' subjects so the teacher needs to put systems in place to ensure that both boys and girls have equal access to the curriculum through participation in discussion and access to both mathematics and ICT equipment.

The delivery of the lesson

A range of teaching strategies should be employed to meet the different needs of individuals. This includes the subject content, the activities that are chosen and the teaching methodology that is used. This means that the teacher needs to use a range of teaching and learning approaches both effectively and with confidence. The teacher should have planned for these at the planning stage, although the more experienced practitioner will have a range of strategies to use intuitively once the lesson has begun. The lesson will be well paced, particularly important where ICT is used, as it ensures that the lesson does not 'drift'. It needs to be purposeful, in that it gives the pupils sufficient time to complete their tasks, but not so long that it loses the momentum of the lesson. Teaching and learning is always that much more effective if it is sharp and focussed. Additionally, high-quality teaching time is always at a premium in schools, but especially so if an intensively timetabled ICT suite is being used. Therefore it is equally important that the teaching is rigorous, so that the teacher ensures that learning is taking place. This will be through the use of ongoing assessment, which takes place through the use of sharp and focussed open-ended questioning, explained below. This ensures that the children are making progress at every stage of the lesson. Given that the teacher will be working to a national framework, it is important to ensure that all teaching time is being used productively.

The importance of interactive teaching

The best lessons are those that make extensive use of interactive teaching and learning. In the introduction we stressed the importance of ensuring that the children interact with the computer, but it is just as important that the children interact with the teacher. So in the same way that the child must not become a passive recipient of the information on the computer screen, they must not become passive recipients of information passed on from the teacher! The best way to ensure this is to employ investigative teaching activities that necessitate the children finding things out for themselves. The teachers can then support this approach by asking the children a range of open-ended questions, examples of which can include:

- What have you discovered? Tell me about it.
- Why do you think you have got those results?
- What would happen if ...?

This line of questioning is ideal for detailed formative assessment, to determine the extent to which children have learnt; it is a powerful means of extending children's thinking and consequently their learning.

Selecting appropriate resources

For very good school organisational reasons, as well as educational ones, the teacher will usually be the one who decides when ICT is to be used within a mathematics context. However, throughout this book we have emphasised the importance of children taking responsibility for their own learning. As far as investigative mathematics and the role of ICT as a tool to assist in mathematical thinking is concerned, the children need to be taught and then encouraged to make key decisions concerning the place and purpose of ICT. This might include key questions such as:

- Is it appropriate to use ICT? The children need to be taught to take responsibility for deciding whether or not ICT should be used to support a particular mathematical investigation. Children are shrewd at evaluating their own work and suggesting how it could be improved, so they should be encouraged to make meaningful decisions about how their work could benefit from the use of ICT. This might be for all or part of the lesson, but however it is used, this approach is entirely in accordance with the requirements of the National Curriculum for ICT in England.

- If so, in which context should it be employed? Once the children have decided that it would be relevant to use ICT, and that a 'value-added' component would be provided, they then need to determine at which point in the investigation it needs to be used. Is it to capture an image at the start of an investigation, or is it to handle and manipulate raw data in the middle of it? Is it to be used to present the findings of an investigation that has been completed without the use of ICT? Whatever the context, the children need to be taught to make these kinds of higher-level decisions, and the organisation and management of the lesson will need to be flexible to accommodate this. Of course the teacher will already have a preconceived idea as to what she or he wishes the children to do as far as ICT is concerned, so skilled questioning will be necessary to steer the children in the right direction. This means that both teacher and lesson plan need to be flexible enough to accommodate this approach.

- Which hardware should be used? This is a good example of the teacher needing be able to predict which pieces of equipment the children may require prior to the start of the lesson, so both teacher and pupil need to think ahead. If digital cameras are to be used then they will need to be booked and the batteries checked.

- Which software is the most appropriate to effectively support the activity or task being completed? We have already discussed the importance of making judicious evaluations of software in the previous chapter, as in many ways this is the most challenging question of all. We are not suggesting that pupils decide which particular software package is used – this needs to be done by the teacher in the same way that they would select any other educational resource. However, even quite young pupils can make informed judgements as to which type of application should be used for a particular purpose. For example, a key element of mathematics and ICT is handling data, which in turn directly entails the major decision of whether to use a database or a spreadsheet. Although this is dealt with in greater depth elsewhere in this book, it is worth mentioning it here. A database is used for the storing and sorting of information; a spreadsheet is used for manipulating numbers and information. But a spreadsheet can also be used as a database! Which one do you use and why?

Although some teachers may be reluctant to pass over this level of control to the children, it should be remembered that both the level descriptors and the attainment targets of the ICT National Curriculum document for England require the children to make these sorts of decisions – even at Key Stages 1 and 2. A good teacher is often a teacher who is prepared to take a risk when teaching – not being afraid to let the children have a say in their own learning is a good example of this. This ownership can be liberating for a child and can provide teachers with new insights into the way that their children learn, and what type of people they are.

Organising teaching and learning with a computer

The majority of primary school teachers are particularly skilled when delivering a mathematics lesson. However, the perceived difficulties of using ICT in a lesson can prevent some teachers from exploiting the power that it offers to the full. The next sections will attempt to assist teachers in overcoming any misgivings that they may have about using the technology.

As this is a mathematics, rather than an ICT, lesson, its main focus must remain on the key mathematics objectives, with the ICT embedded in both planning and the lesson. The role of the ICT is to support the mathematics being taught by the teacher and learned by the child through the provision of the 'value-added' element. Ideally, the mathematics and ICT components should be taught together to ensure that the ICT is used within the correct context. It is also advantageous to have the ICT resources to hand, to ensure that it is integrated with the investigation, any other ongoing classroom activities and is near other resources so that research and all aspects of collaborative learning can easily occur. However, due to organisational reasons within the school this may not be possible. In many schools the ICT resources are located in a timetabled ICT suite that can only be accessed at certain times during the day or week. Therefore there needs to be consideration of how this limited time can be fully utilised.

Example scenario

So how might a lesson and sequence of lessons where ICT is to be used develop? Let us look at the following example that suggests how this could be done.

A class of 30 Year 3 children are to complete a traffic survey. They will be organised into six groups of five and, accompanied by a responsible adult, will spend 20 minutes recording the traffic on a nearby road. They will then return to the classroom, look at their data and enter their findings into a computer for subsequent interrogation and analysis. This will take four lessons and will be organised as follows:

- Lesson One: To discuss the collection of the data and to design and produce tally charts for completion.
- Lesson Two: To collect the data itself.
- Lesson Three: To organise the data for entry into the computer.
- Lesson Four: To enter the data, and then analyse the subsequent information.

Lesson One will begin with the teacher describing to the class the place and purpose of the task. There will then be a discussion where the teacher will discuss with the children how the traffic flows might be observed and then recorded. Following a focussed discussion, the teacher will then teach the class how to produce a tally chart. Suggestions for the layout and content might even come from the children themselves – they may even produce their own on a computer. It should have different categories, or fields, to allow the children to record different vehicles such as cars, buses, lorries, motorcycles, bicycles etc. This will need to be discussed carefully with the children at this point, ensuring that all groups are doing the activity properly, and that they are doing the same thing so that comparisons can be made.

Lesson Two will involve the children going out with an adult to observe and record the traffic flows. This might be the same adult taking each group out in turn, or it might involve six adults each taking a group. The first method is better, as over the course of a day six different 20-minute periods can be recorded and a more complete picture built up. The adult can also ensure that the children are tackling the task in similar ways that will ensure that it remains a fair test and that each group is learning the same thing.

Lesson Three will involve the children returning to the classroom and preparing their data for entry to the computer. This is the first point that the data handling package to be used should be introduced into the computer. Indeed, it will be possible to hold a discussion with the more able children to determine which type of data handling package should be used. There is a possibility for misconception here, in that some children (and indeed adults!) will have difficulty in deciding whether a database or a spreadsheet should be used. In fact it should be a spreadsheet rather than a database, as there is only one record involved (the traffic survey), although there will of course be several fields (the different vehicles). This discussion enables the children to prepare a simple spreadsheet to handle the information. Using a simple package such as *Number Box*, an excellent primary school spreadsheet that is part of the *Black Cat Toolbox*, currently published by Granada Learning, the children, together with some adult help, can actually set the spreadsheet up for themselves. Alternatively, the teacher can do this (which makes consistency at the planning and data collection stage doubly important), which may benefit those children who have special needs. This will mean that there may only need to be three lessons, as there will be no need for the children to prepare their own spreadsheets. Indeed, *Number Box* has a quick sheets facility that enables the user to set up different spreadsheets for a range of uses quickly and easily.

Lesson Four involves the children entering their data into the database and analysing the resulting information. Although they are grouped in sixes, experience has taught the authors that when working at computers, pairs tends to be the optimum group size for an activity of this nature as it is easier to ensure that the effort is equally shared. Therefore, they may work in three lots of pairs, and then work as a six under adult supervision to analyse the information. This will involve the children predicting which vehicles they think will be the most common, entering the data into the spreadsheet and then interpreting the data. The interpretation will almost certainly require the production of a range of bar charts to enable the children to look for trends.

Although this may signal the end of the investigation, the children can then write up their findings on a package such as *Microsoft Word*, and can cut and paste their graphs into this. They can also present their findings to the other members of the class, perhaps using digital images in a *Microsoft PowerPoint* presentation along with the graphs. This is visually very striking and represents a powerful means for pupils to present the results of their mathematical investigations.

The next sections of this chapter will describe how the teacher can deliver the above lessons where the ICT resources are organised in different ways, namely:
- Teaching mathematics in the ICT suite and
- Teaching mathematics away from the ICT suite.

Teaching mathematics in the ICT suite

One of the inherent problems of teaching in an ICT suite is the perception that this particular learning environment can unconsciously encourage the computer to take precedence over the subject. In a room such as this, the computer becomes the focus of all activities, and therefore it can be difficult for both teacher and pupil to appreciate that they are part of a mathematics lesson. With the computers dominating this environment it can be slightly intimidating and the mathematics element can seem completely divorced from the ICT. For a start the room is laid out in a different way. The children are seated at computers in such a way that they may not be able to see the teacher or the board at the front of the room. In turn, the teacher may not be able to see the children's faces; they may be obscured by the computers, or may have their backs to the teacher. Therefore there may be a requirement for teachers to change their teaching style and their classroom management and organisation techniques, which will need to be made explicit at the planning stage. Teaching in an ICT suite is more akin to teaching a practical lesson such as art, physical education, or music. As we have mentioned before, this can represent a challenge; is not difficult, but is different.

So the teacher in our traffic survey example must remember at all times that the purpose of using the suite is to enable the children to enter the data they have collected from their survey into the computer for subsequent interrogation, graphing and analysis. Although these are discrete ICT skills as detailed by the ICT National Curriculum document for England, this remains a mathematics lesson as that is the context in which ICT is being used. In order to maximise the actual 'hands-on' time, the preliminary discussion, fieldwork and observations, and the recording and predicting, will have been completed prior to entering the ICT suite. Likewise the plenary should be completed back in the classroom afterwards.

At this stage consideration also needs to be given to other related issues including:

- Who turns the computers on? This may be an ICT technician, another adult such as the ICT Co-ordinator or a classroom learning assistant, or the teacher who is about to use the room. It might even be the children, who then log themselves on to the computer and the network. Whoever does this, the children must not become distracted from the main purpose of the lesson: to decide which software package to use and to enter the collected data into it.
- Who troubleshoots small problems? This includes changing ink cartridges, fixing printers that have gone offline or changing batteries for digital cameras. The class teacher may have the technical knowledge and

understanding to do this, but when teaching a class of 30-plus pupils, this is difficult. Nor should they need to, as teachers are employed to teach, not fix technical problems. However, if these problems are not sorted they can disrupt the delivery of the lesson. The children must be in a position to print off their spreadsheets and graphs, even if these are first drafts, to enable group discussion about their findings.

■ What if there are not enough computers for the whole class? This is an important organisational and management issue in some schools, especially smaller ones, and necessitates a range of strategies. This will normally entail the class being divided into two or more groups, which instantly creates a new problem: the need for two teachers. We have already stated that it is advantageous for pupils to work in pairs at the computer, so this may be the best solution to this problem. It is always important to ensure that solutions such as these are done for educational, rather than organisational, reasons. There must be sufficient space between the computers to allow the children the correct amount of elbow room and also provide space for any mathematical equipment and work books that will be needed as part of the lesson.

Teaching mathematics away from the ICT suite

Ideally ICT should be used where the mathematics is being taught, and this will usually mean away from the ICT suite. This, almost by definition, means that the lesson is delivered in the 'usual' classroom, or as practical work either outside in the school grounds or perhaps even away from the school, such as on a field trip or a visit to a museum.

The main advantage of using the pupil's usual classroom is that the children will feel secure as it is their normal learning environment, but at a more pragmatic level it is where most of the teaching takes place. As a result of this, most of the mathematical resources are located here and both the teacher and learners will be able to use them in a natural, integrated way. The teacher will be able to use open-ended questioning to enable the children to decide for themselves what equipment they will need; unintended learning outcomes may well result from a teacher's intuitive responses to the children's work. However, many schools only have a core provision of ICT computers, which are located centrally in an ICT suite rather than dispersed around the school. The advantage of this is that whole-class teaching can take place where children have sufficient access to ICT equipment at the same time – important for whole-class teaching – but the disadvantage is that, as detailed above, resources are not readily to hand. It is important that schools consider the relative advantages and disadvantages of locating ICT resources as either a core or peripheral provision. Many schools are in the fortunate position of being able to have both – computers centrally located in an ICT suite and in the classroom. Admittedly, classroom computers are often older computers that cannot be networked – which in turn means no Internet or e-mail access – but these can still be a very useful resource, regardless of the relative age of the equipment concerned. It should also be remembered that ICT equipment can also include digital cameras or laptops, which can be used anywhere. Indeed, where wireless networking is concerned, modern laptops can even be used outside and still provide access to the Internet. This is particularly useful if the children are following an investigation, perhaps in another part of the school or even outdoors, and need Internet access. They can also download images from digital cameras and share them over the wireless network to other parts of the school, as long as these are part of the same network.

Teaching the lesson with one computer

Even now, when most primary schools have modern and well-equipped ICT suites, the authors are still asked by trainees and teachers how to teach when there is access to only one machine in the classroom. Although most also have access to suites, there thankfully remains a willingness on the part of the teacher to incorporate ICT into everyday practice. This of course is to be encouraged, but it does create some organisational issues.

With some thought and forward planning, using the one computer in a classroom can be advantageous to the teacher. It can provide the teacher with the opportunity to teach the children how to use a particular piece of software prior to using the ICT suite. This ensures that the weekly hour in the ICT suite can be utilised more effectively, by ensuring that the bulk of the time is 'hands-on', rather than the teacher talking or the children engaged away from the computers. With such a limited amount of 'hands-on' time anyway, it is crucial that every minute in the ICT suite is maximised. Teaching and the plenary can occur in the classroom – the natural teaching environment – with the ICT taking place in its natural environment, the ICT suite. Therefore, as far as our traffic survey example is concerned, the teacher will be able to introduce the activities in the children's classroom, including the use of ICT at every step of the way. When the children reach the point where they need to work intensively at the computer, they can do this in the ICT suite. At a push, this can be done in the classroom too, but this can prove to be very time consuming, and often puts teachers off using these more extended tasks with their classes.

So how should the teacher organise and manage teaching and learning where there is only access to one computer?

■ For whole-class teaching with a single computer the teacher should seat the children around the monitor. If it has a large screen, so much the better. If there is only a standard monitor, then the input should occur in groups. Some could even be delivered by the classroom learning assistant.

■ The input should only be in very general terms – it is always a good idea to let the children explore new software for themselves – with the key features of the software being demonstrated, and the place and purpose of it being explained. We have already discussed the fact that, if it is good intuitive software, then the children will more quickly understand how it works, and will have a sense of ownership over it. They will get a 'feel' for the way that it works and what it can offer them in their given learning situation. In our example the teacher would at this point explain how to use the spreadsheet software and how to enter the data into it. At a later date, the teacher would then demonstrate to the children how to sort, search and analyse the information. Ideally this should occur in the classroom rather than the ICT suite, so as to utilise the time most effectively and to provide a meaningful context in which the mathematics can be taught.

■ If the teacher wishes the children to use a single computer in the classroom, then there is an effective method that can be employed: having explained how the software works, the teacher should select two of the more able children in the class to begin work on the computer. One of the pair could 'drive' the mouse, whilst the second child could contribute by providing the collected data or, in other contexts, knowledge and ideas. In this way, one child does not become an isolated user at the screen, as there is collaborative learning through the sharing of ideas.

■ If the children are working on individual tasks, perhaps producing some mathematical pictures on a graphics package, the second child is able to learn about the workings of the program by watching the user and through contributing ideas as to how the work could be improved. When the child who is 'driving' the mouse completes their work, she or he saves or prints it and then moves aside. The second child moves into the 'hot seat' and another child comes to act as helper. It is important to change this 'elite' group from time to time, but the fact that more able children are being used at this stage will ensure that they themselves will be able to sort out any problems that arise. This will ensure that the teacher can concentrate on getting the remainder of the class settled and on task, before moving across to see how the children who are using the computer are getting on. As a result the pupil–teacher interaction will be concerned with discussion of the task rather than technical aspects of ICT, so the quality of the pupil–teacher interaction will be higher. From a classroom management perspective, this tactic also ensures that the teacher gets a vital couple of minutes to manage the transition from the demonstration to the commencement of work. The first couple of minutes are crucial to the success of the ensuing lesson.

A spreadsheet case study

Our thanks to Mrs Miriam Foster and the children at Westbury Primary School, Letchworth Garden City, Hertfordshire.

The mixed class in this case study has 32 children from Years 4 and 5. They have a wide range of abilities and experience.

All the children were asked to imagine that they were going to give a party for 20 friends, but had only £20 to spend on food for the party. After much discussion, and a good deal of writing of notes and even some rough calculations, the children decided what kinds of food they would need, and the individual prices for each item.

The remainder of the work was carried out using the spreadsheet program on the school's RM computers. All the children completed their own spreadsheet, and examples of these are shown in Figures 2.1, 2.2 and 2.3. Although they are self-explanatory, experienced teachers will recognise the amount of work that

	A	B	C	D	E	F	G	H	I	J
1	drinks	crisps	cakes	sausage rs	pizza	sandwiches	Ice-cream	Burger	smarties	nuts
2	£0.30	£0.20	£0.10	£0.40	£1.50	£0.50	£1.00	£2.00	£4.00	£5.00
3	3	2	3	2	4	4	2	3	5	3
4	0.9	0.4	0.3	0.8	6	2	4	6	20	15
5										
6										
7										
8										

Figure 2.1 Amber and Lucy's spreadsheet. These children have successfully inserted pound signs and decimal points into the cost-per-unit row to make them appear as money.

	A	B	C	D	E	F	G
1	crisps	cakes	pizza	sandwitche	nuts	sugasrolls	drink
2	0.25	0.9	0.8	0.53			----
3	8	2	3	2	20		
4	£2	£3.50	£2.40	£1.60			
5							
6							
7							

Figure 2.2 Dee and Paige's spreadsheet. They have inserted pound signs in the cumulative totals of each column.

	A	B	C	D	E	F	G	H	I
1	cake	pizza	nuts	sandwiches	sausage	crisps	drinks	sweets	cost
2	0.90	0.80	0.10	0.53	0.17	0.25	0.30	0.05	
3	6	2	10	3	2	6	6	35	
4	5.4	1.6	1	1.59	0.34	1.5	1.8	1.75	14.98

Figure 2.3 Louisa's spreadsheet. She has added an additional column at the extreme right-hand end displaying the total cost of the food for the party.

would be required for a class of this size and complexity to do all the work 'by hand'. Of course, at the start of the project, some of it was. It is necessary for as many of the children as possible to understand the mathematics required to make these calculations, just as it is for them to recognise the simple mathematics of a pocket calculator. However, by handing over the mechanics to a computer, the children were able to complete the calculations in a sensible time, and find the motivation to attempt a more complex series of calculations for later work.

This project was designed to meet the data-handling requirements of the Numeracy Hour, although with the extra work involving the 'raw' mathematical calculations as well as the detailed discussion within the class, a good deal more interesting work was completed than that needed for this one basic requirement.

Conclusion

Hopefully this chapter will have illustrated that the delivery of a lesson where mathematics and ICT are used can be relatively straightforward. As we have mentioned elsewhere, teaching with ICT is not difficult, but it is different, especially if it takes place in the potentially alien environment of the ICT suite. However, teachers should not overreact by attempting to change their teaching strategies completely, as this could leave them using strategies that are unfamiliar and, as a consequence, their teaching will be less effective. After all, good teaching is good teaching, regardless of subject or location. It might be necessary to modify their teaching approach to take into account the extra element that using ICT inevitably brings. This should not be seen as a threat but as a challenge, as it will enable teacher and learner to successfully harness the power of the computer.

Bibliography

DfEE/QCA, *The National Curriculum for England*, HMSO, London, 1999.

Chapter 3

Using an interactive whiteboard

Even in a period of great technological advances, one of the most remarkable pieces of ICT hardware to become available to education in recent years is the interactive whiteboard. This piece of equipment alone has the power to completely revolutionise the way that teachers teach, and learners learn. This chapter will describe what an interactive whiteboard is, what it can do, and discuss the contribution that it can make to the teaching and learning of mathematics in the primary school.

What is an interactive whiteboard?

In order to use an interactive whiteboard you need:

- The board itself, usually fixed to the wall or mounted on a portable stand.
- A computer to both run the board and demonstrate different types of software.
- A data projector to project the computer's screen image onto the board.
- Software to run the board (usually supplied with it).

As the name suggests, an interactive whiteboard is based upon the traditional whiteboard that is widely used in many primary classrooms, where the user writes upon a whiteboard with a dry wipe marker pen. This can then be erased with a dry, soft cloth using a specially formulated spray to remove stubborn ink marks. Although an interactive whiteboard looks very similar to its traditional counterpart, and some makes of board even allow the user to write directly on them with a dry wipe pen, there the similarity ends. It is directly connected to a computer through a long cable via a serial or USB port, and the computer's screen image is projected onto the board through a data projector. When the board is calibrated to work with the computer, the user touches the relevant parts of the projected image on the whiteboard and the computer responds in the same way that it would if the user was controlling it with a mouse. This means that the teacher or child can stand at the front of the class and can demonstrate a concept or idea, or give a presentation, perhaps using *Microsoft PowerPoint*, harnessing the full power of a computer but without having to actually stand next to it. A simple tap on the board moves to the next slide or actions the next response from the hardware or software. Additionally, if the teacher is explaining the features of a piece of software, then electronic lines can be drawn on the board as an overlay on the screen image to highlight key features.

Everybody, even in quite large rooms, can clearly and easily see the boards, which are usually available in three different sizes. They have three main roles as teaching aids. They can be used to:
- Demonstrate how individual pieces of software work.
- Display a presentation.
- Act as an electronic version of the traditional whiteboard or flipchart.

When used effectively, there is more to an interactive whiteboard than simply electronically mimicking something from a previous generation purely for the sake of it. As it is computer operated, it means that all of the powerful functions of the computer are now available to a teacher when teaching or demonstrating. A user can quickly cover a traditional blackboard or whiteboard during the course of the lesson with writing or diagrams, which often means that the teacher has to rub out material perhaps before the children have finished reading it, or before the teacher has fully made the appropriate teaching points. Difficulties can also arise if there is a need to continue the lesson at a later time or date. In a primary school classroom the teacher will almost certainly need the board for lessons involving other areas of the curriculum, or may even have to move rooms to enable another class to use it. We have all seen boards in classrooms with 'Please leave' written on them, but of course this is not always practical. One key advantage of the interactive whiteboard is that it allows the user to save individual screens and flip charts, which can then be reloaded and developed at any point in the future. This flexibility also allows the teacher to save the material onto a portable storage device such as a floppy disk, zip disk or CD-ROM and then move it to another computer that is connected to an interactive whiteboard. This is particularly advantageous if the school is fortunate enough to possess more than one whiteboard, or if for any reason the teacher needs to visit another site. This flexibility enables teachers to extend and develop their own teaching.

Calibrating the interactive whiteboard

Although there are several manufacturers of interactive whiteboards, the example discussed here is the *Activboard*, which is manufactured by Promethean, using the *Activstudio* software. This particular make of board is controlled by the user through the use of a stylus, an implement that looks very similar to a pen. Touching the board with the end of the stylus has a similar effect to left-clicking on a computer screen with a mouse. Pressing a button on the barrel of the stylus causes the board to replicate the effect of right-clicking with a mouse.

Once the interactive whiteboard has been set up and connected to the computer, the next step is to calibrate it. This enables the whiteboard to match itself to the corresponding screen area on the computer. Because the projected image of the computer's screen is dependent on the distance of the data projector from the board itself, the image has to be matched to the active area of the interactive whiteboard. This is done by launching the calibration software that is supplied with the board, either in the usual way from the programs menu, or through clicking on a dot in the bottom left-hand corner of the whiteboard itself. When this happens, the user is presented with the screen illustrated in Figure 3.1.

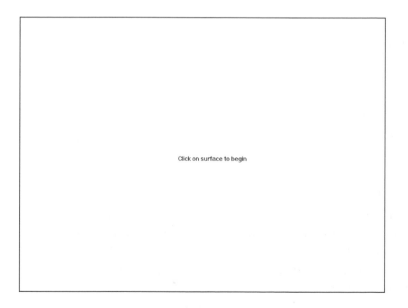

Click on surface to begin

Figure 3.1 The first calibration screen as used by the Promethean *Activboard*.

When prompted by the command 'Click on surface to begin', the user clicks on the board with the stylus and the next screen, illustrated in Figure 3.2 appears.

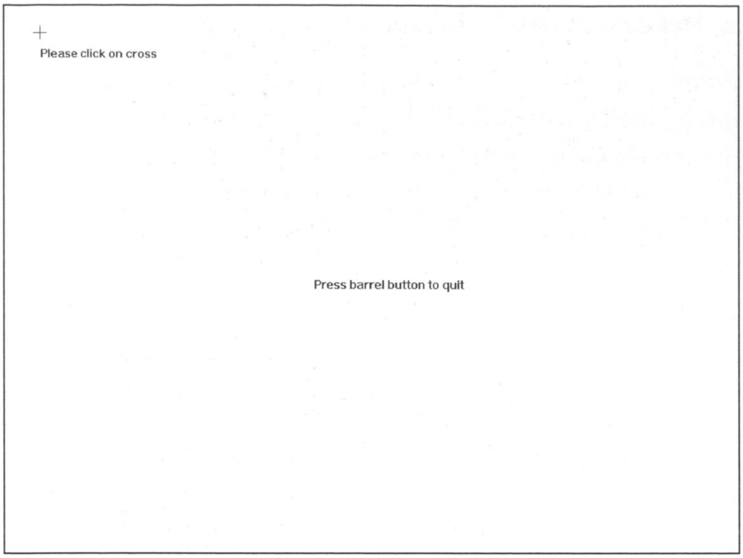

Figure 3.2 The second calibration screen from the Promethean *Activboard*.

The user then clicks on the middle of the cross in the top left corner of the screen. The user is subsequently presented with three further screens each with one cross in each of the remaining corners. This sets up the active area of the whiteboard, so that the arrow on the computer screen matches the position of the stylus on the board. The *Activboard* is now ready for use to display and run presentations and pieces of software.

Using the interactive whiteboard

Throughout this book we have continually stressed the importance of pupil and teacher interacting with each other as well as with the computer. We discussed above three main ways in which the interactive whiteboard can be used to assist teaching and learning. The first two ways, demonstrating how individual pieces of software work and displaying a presentation, can certainly assist teaching and learning, but it is the third way, extending the traditional whiteboard or flipchart, which offers the most exciting possibilities. For as the name suggests, this is where genuinely interactive teaching can take place. This is the point where the teacher interacts with the board, the hardware and software and, above all, the pupils.

In order to access all of the features and functions that the interactive whiteboard has to offer, the user needs to launch the *Activstudio* software that is supplied with the board. When this happens a menu appears in the right-hand corner of the screen (see Figure 3.3).

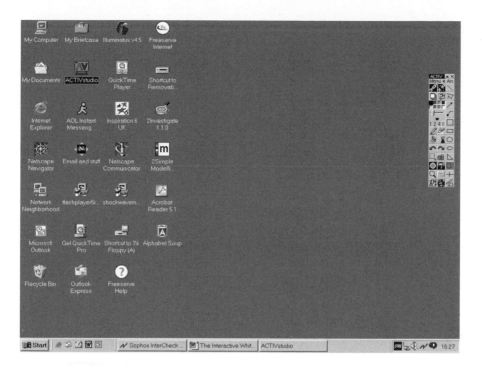

Figure 3.3 Screenshot of a *Windows 98* desktop complete with *Activstudio* menu on the right-hand side of the screen.

By clicking on a range of icons with the stylus the user can access different features. These include:

- Drawing tools – allow the drawing of a range of lines and regular shapes;
- Flipchart – allows the user to electronically 'write' on the board;
- Annotation tool – puts a 'transparent layer' over the screen which allows the user to highlight key features;
- Pen colours – several colours can be selected;
- Pen width control – as can the width;
- Free hand pen – to write/draw on the board;
- Highlighter – to highlight key features;
- Board rubber – to erase material on the board;
- Select tool – to select areas of the screen;
- Camera tool – to copy/paste parts of the screen;
- Spotlight and reveal tools – to show only parts of the screen;
- Magnifier tools – to enlarge parts of the screen;
- Keyboard tool – to type letters on the screen;
- Handwriting recognition tool – to convert the user's handwriting into a computer font;
- Map of Great Britain;

■ Background screens, including musical staves, squared paper, clock faces and shapes.

The interactive whiteboard can be used for highlighting key features and illustrating main teaching points through the use of the annotation tool. This allows the user to draw or write on to the projected screen image, which is particularly useful if the teacher wishes to emphasise a particular teaching point. Illustrated in Figure 3.4 is a spreadsheet created in *Number Box*, a program that is part of the *Black Cat Toolbox*, published by Granada Learning.

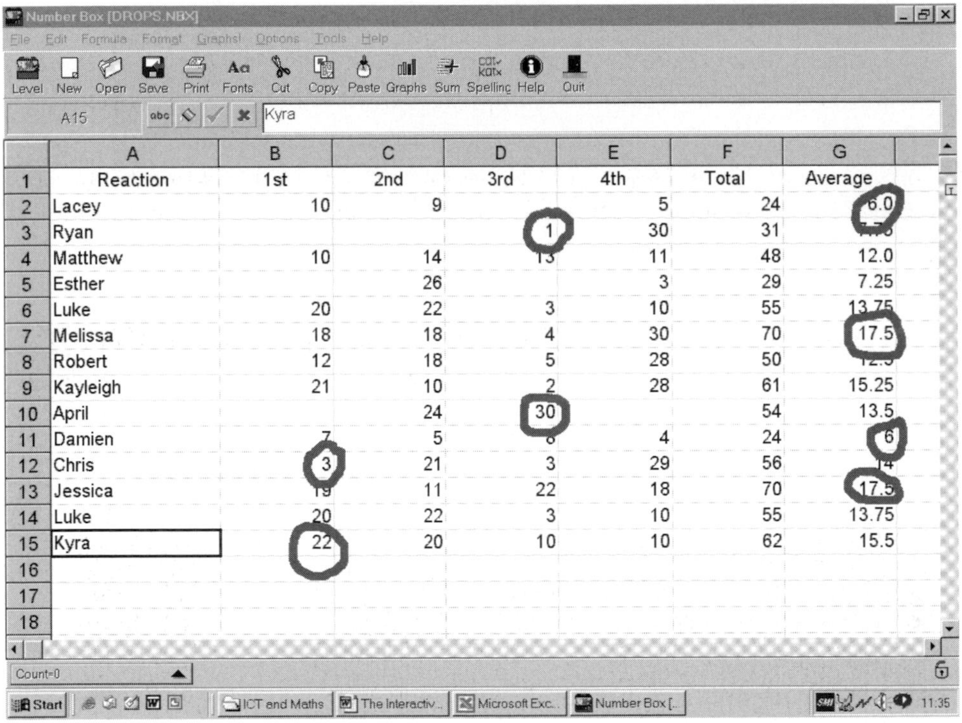

Figure 3.4 Children's reaction times recorded in a spreadsheet in the *Number Box* program, with fastest and slowest reaction times highlighted through the interactive whiteboard.

Here the children have tested their reactions by catching a falling ruler. The children worked in pairs, with one child dropping the ruler without warning and the other child trying to catch it as quickly as possible. Where the fingers catch the ruler the measurement is taken. The results were then entered into the spreadsheet projected onto the interactive whiteboard. Using the stylus and the annotation tool the teacher has then illustrated the quickest and slowest reactions. The pen colour and width could be changed. A special highlighter tool could also have been used, where the *Activstudio* software can mimic the effect of a highlighter pen (see Figures 3.6). The spreadsheet could form the basis for discussion in the class with key questions being asked, such as:

■ Who had the fastest reactions?

■ Who had the slowest reactions?

■ Has the person with the fastest reaction time got the best average? If so why, if not, then why not?

■ Has the person with the slowest reaction time got the worst average? If so why, if not, then why not? (Of course these questions need to be asked in a sensitive manner).

The teacher may then decide to graph the results and highlight the key features on the graph. First, the teacher would highlight the area to be graphed, which in this case is not all of the spreadsheet but just the 'drops' and the average, not the total. The two separate areas of highlighting are completed by highlighting one block, then holding down the control key and highlighting the next area (see Figure 3.5).

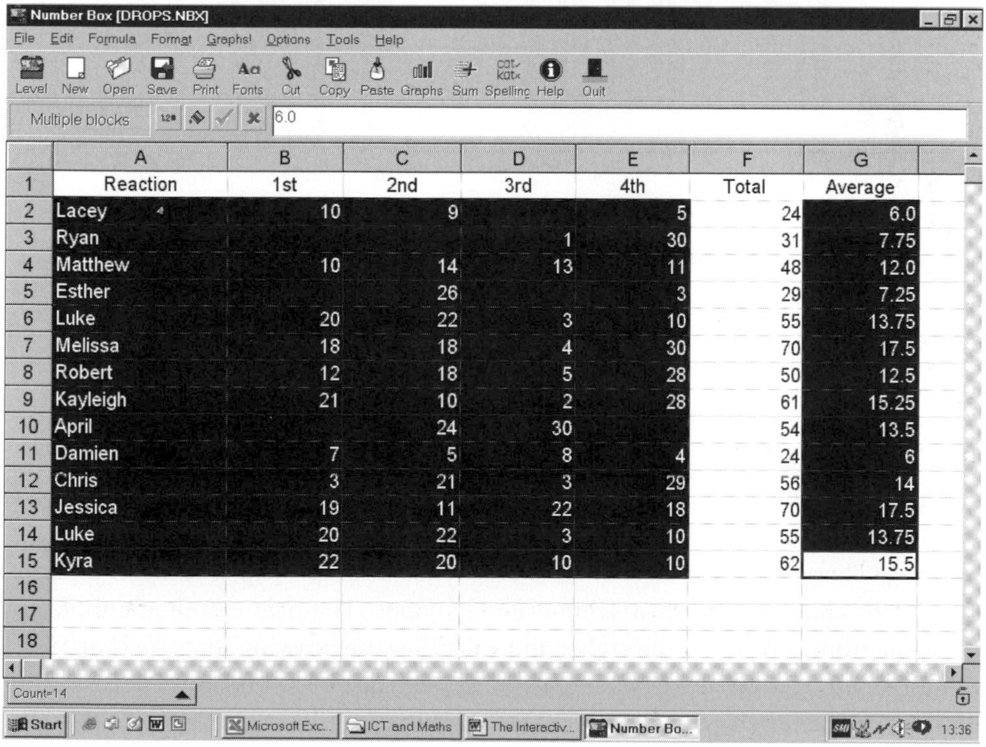

	A	B	C	D	E	F	G
1	Reaction	1st	2nd	3rd	4th	Total	Average
2	Lacey	10	9		5	24	6.0
3	Ryan			1	30	31	7.75
4	Matthew	10	14	13	11	48	12.0
5	Esther		26		3	29	7.25
6	Luke	20	22	3	10	55	13.75
7	Melissa	18	18	4	30	70	17.5
8	Robert	12	18	5	28	50	12.5
9	Kayleigh	21	10	2	28	61	15.25
10	April		24	30		54	13.5
11	Damien	7	5	8	4	24	6
12	Chris	3	21	3	29	56	14
13	Jessica	19	11	22	18	70	17.5
14	Luke	20	22	3	10	55	13.75
15	Kyra	22	20	10	10	62	15.5

Figure 3.5 The drop results and average highlighted on a *Number Box* spreadsheet.

The teacher then clicks on the Graphs icon on the toolbar and selects Bar 2 to get the resulting graph, as illustrated in Figure 3.6. Using the annotation and highlighter tools, the teacher can then ring or mark with a cross the fastest and slowest reactions and averages. The teacher has highlighted the appropriate names and averages to further emphasise the main teaching points.

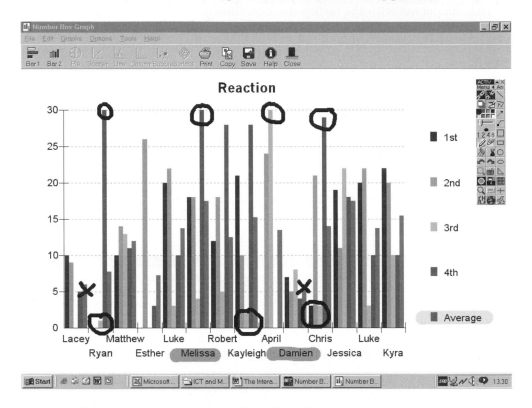

Figure 3.6 The drop results and average highlighted on a *Number Box* graph.

This idea of the teacher being able to instantly interact with the board, computer and the class can be further developed by using a range of software resources that are part of the overall whiteboard package. There are a number of templates included that can be used as a background to support a range of mathematics teaching. These include different sizes and types of graph paper, number squares, clock faces and two- and three-dimensional shapes. The user can then annotate these electronically using the stylus and selecting the drawing tools, perhaps though labelling, drawing or tracing over existing outlines. These are accessed by clicking on the flipchart option and then selecting from a new menu on the right-hand side of the screen. This menu is known as the Tile Menu, and at this point the new user can select the templates from 'default' (a plain white screen), plain colours or tiles. There are literally dozens of these, some more appropriate for primary mathematics than others, but interactive whiteboards are designed to support all areas of the curriculum at all key stages. Some of the templates that are relevant to primary mathematics are illustrated in Figures 3.7 to 3.18.

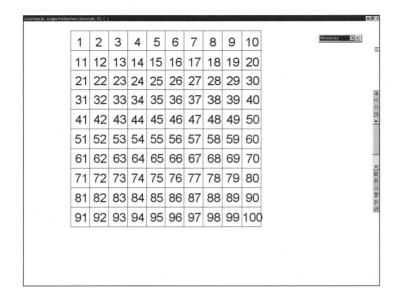

Figure 3.7 100 square. As with the examples above, the teacher or child could highlight individual numbers or number patterns, such as the five times table. This could serve as the basis for wider class discussion.

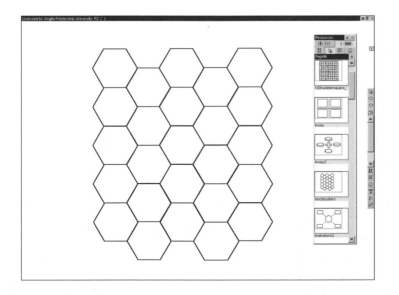

Figure 3.8 Blockbusters – a tessellating pattern of hexagons. A whole range of shapes can be dragged and dropped onto the flipchart to investigate whether or not that particular shape can tessellate.

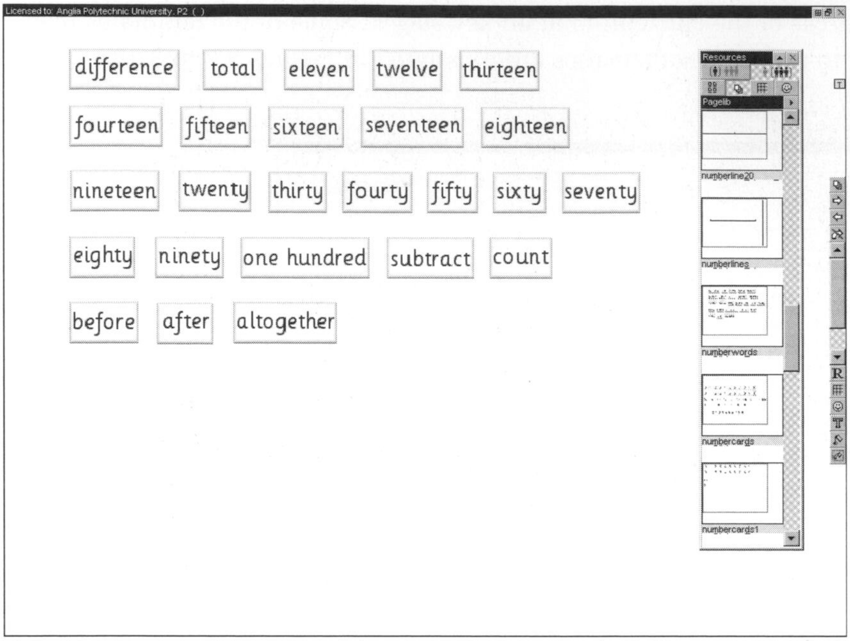

Licensed to: Anglia Polytechnic University. P2 ( )
difference
total
eleven
twelve
thirteen
fourteen
fifteen
sixteen
seventeen
eighteen
nineteen
twenty
thirty
fourty
fifty
sixty
seventy
eighty
ninety
one hundred
subtract
count
before
after
altogether
Resources
Pagelib
numberline20
numberlines
numberwords
numbercards
numbercards1

Figure 3.9 Number words.

Licensed to: Anglia Polytechnic University. P1 ( )
Resources

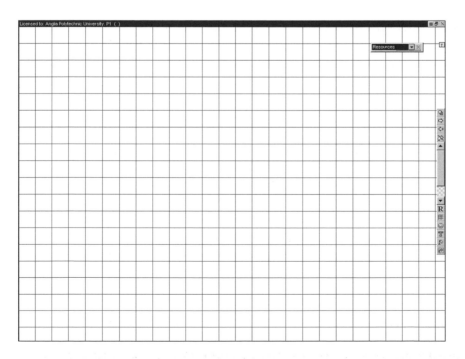

Figure 3.10 Squared paper. This is available in several different sizes and colours and can be used for activities such as 'hand drawing' graphs with the stylus, or for drawing vectors.

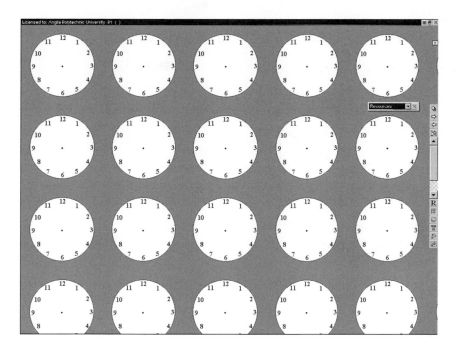

Figure 3.11 Clock face stamps. The user, whether it be teacher or child, can draw hands on to the faces using the arrow tools and even drag them round into different positions using the stylus.

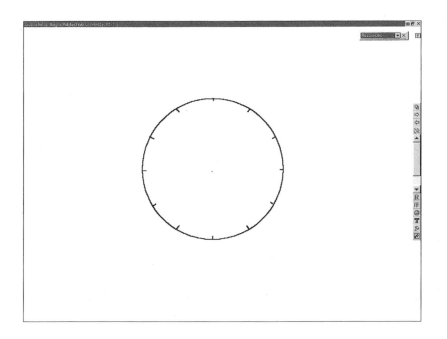

Figure 3.12 A blank clock face. This could be used by the teacher or the pupils to draw hands on, to diplay any permutation of times

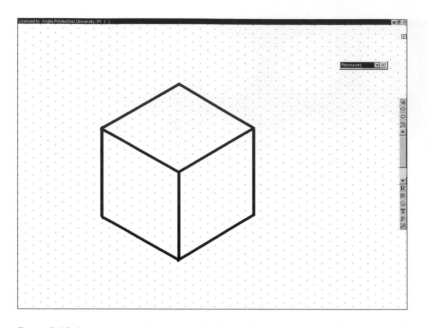

Figure 3.13 Isometric graph paper with three-dimensional cube drawn using the straight line drawing tool. Increasingly complex shapes in three dimensions can be drawn using this template as a guide.

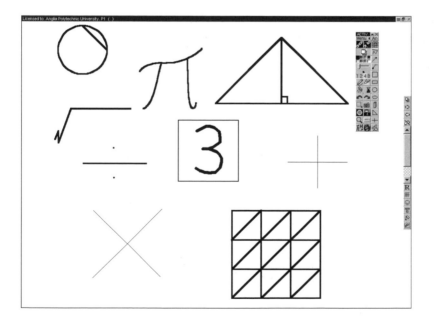

Figure 3.14 A selection of mathematical shapes and symbols that could be useful in a number of different mathematical contexts.

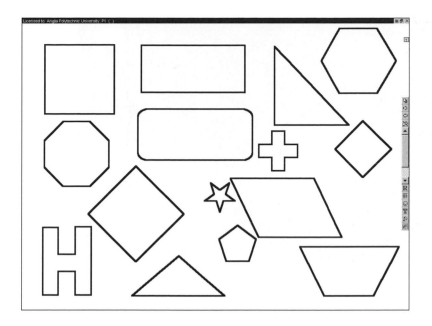

Figure 3.15 A range of two-dimensional shapes available to the user. They can be adjusted for size and transformed by holding the stylus down, and then by dragging it around the board. They can be rotated by right-clicking over the required shape and selecting the desired action.

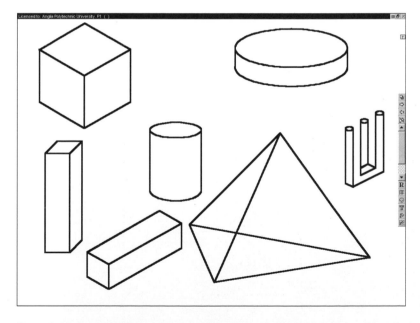

Figure 3.16 A range of three-dimensional shapes available to the user. As with the two-dimensional shapes, they can be adjusted for size and transformed by holding the stylus down, and then by dragging or stretching around the board. They can be rotated by right-clicking over the required shape and selecting the desired action.

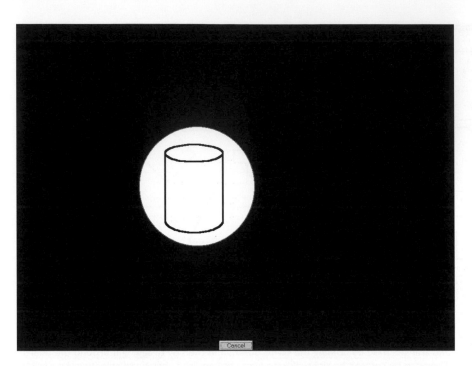

Figure 3.17 The spotlight feature enables the user to show individual parts of the board.

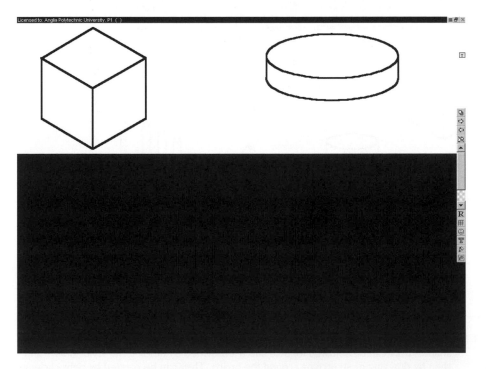

Figure 3.18 The reveal function enables the user to progressively reveal parts of the whiteboard, in much the same way that previous generations of teachers used to reveal slides on overhead projectors.

The true flexibility of the interactive whiteboard is illustrated by the fact that any particular function can be used with any board background. This includes *Microsoft Windows*, any piece of commercially available software and templates that come as part of the *Activstudio* package. A flipchart page can also be used to provide a plain background. It is this level of integration which makes this a powerful and wonderful teaching and learning tool for both teacher and child.

Possibly the most powerful function of all is the software's ability to allow the user to write on the board in flipchart mode, and then convert the user's handwriting into a recognised font. This is particularly useful if the teacher wishes to write something neatly on the board (see Figures 3.19 and 3.20).

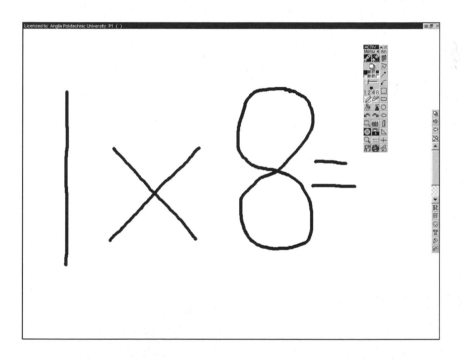

Figure 3.19 Some mathematical handwriting on the interactive whiteboard.

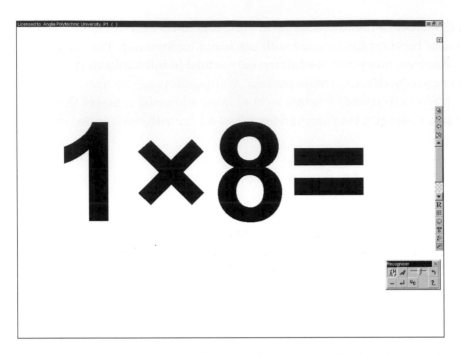

Figure 3.20 Some mathematical handwriting on the interactive whiteboard converted using the handwriting recognition tool. The font style, size and colour can all be chosen, as can the recognition time from 0.5 to 5 seconds. This is Arial font, in black at 200 point.

This is a particularly valuable feature of the Promethean interactive whiteboard. The teacher can write a range of numbers and mathematical words and symbols onto the board by hand, which are instantly converted into a standard font. This means that the teacher does not need to be 'tied' to a computer in order to deliver the lesson, and this is a feature that children will particularly enjoy using. For example, the teacher may want the children to write down a series of number patterns on the board. These can then be converted (although this isn't necessary) and then saved for subsequent use at a later time. The number pattern can be refined, updated and revised. The user may be annotating a diagram or a graph, which again can be converted from quick handwriting into something that is instantly recognisable and extremely neat. This is a motivating factor for children. In the same way that using a word-processing package motivates children who may be reluctant writers or who find the physical act of writing with a pen or pencil difficult, they can now produce writing through the annotating of diagrams or the labelling of graphs, and the computer does all of the difficult work for them. This can have a liberating effect on both teacher and child. The user does not even have to write or draw directly onto the board. A graphics tablet can be used, where the stylus is used on a tablet which is connected to the computer by a remote link, rather than by writing directly onto the board. This is useful for users with special needs who may find moving to the board or reaching up to it difficult, or where the room is crowded and it is easier to take the stylus to the child rather than have the child move to the board.

For an example of a basic use of the interactive whiteboard, refer to the case study in Chapter 1.

Conclusion

There is little doubt that the interactive whiteboard is one of the most impressive resources to be introduced to the primary classroom in recent years. It has the potential to completely transform teaching and learning through the ability to connect teacher, child and computer. It is this ability to harness the power of the computer in an easy yet powerful way that is the most exciting means of all.

Bibliography

For further work on the 'Reactions' case study see:

Williams, J. and Easingwood, N., *ICT and Primary Science*, RoutledgeFalmer, London, 2003.

Chapter 4

The use of floor and screen turtles

Since the introduction of computers into British primary schools during the 1980s, one of the most powerful learning applications available to the teacher has been LOGO. Although essentially a programming language, to simply refer to it as such does not begin to do it justice. Developed by Seymour Papert at the Massachusetts Institute of Technology (MIT) in the 1970s, and discussed in depth in his classic book *Mindstorms* (1980), the philosophy underlying LOGO is to put the child in control of the computer rather than allowing the computer to control the child. As a result, LOGO represents one of the few genuinely 'content-free' applications so far developed for educational use, because the child 'programs' the computer to get a desired response or outcome by entering a series of commands. Although this has to be within the boundaries created by the limitations of the software itself, there is genuine potential for the computer to respond entirely to the wishes of the user.

The concept of LOGO is based around the ability of the user to control a 'turtle', either a real model or a screen simulation. This control is usually done to produce some kind of drawing, by making it move forward and backward for a given number of 'turtle steps', or to the left or the right by degrees. This can be performed with a floor turtle, often known as a Roamer, or smaller and simpler devices such as a Pip or Pixie, or a screen turtle, driven by LOGO software. Floor turtles are programmable toys that have buttons for the child to press so that they move across the floor and change direction. They can also be programmed to make sounds. A screen turtle, which is used in a computer-based LOGO application, is made to move across a computer screen as part of a two-dimensional environment. The turtle can be programmed to draw a line in its wake, thus enabling the user to produce a wide range of drawings, ranging from simple shapes for users in the Foundation stage to complex geometrical patterns at Year 6.

However, LOGO is not simply a drawing or graphics package. Its ability to develop learning comes through the processes that are used to achieve the outcome, not just the outcomes themselves, however important these may be. Although this kind of process-orientated learning has slipped out of fashion in recent years due to the demands and indeed the misinterpretation of the National Curriculum and National Numeracy Strategy in England, LOGO has the potential to create powerful learning outcomes that are nevertheless entirely in accordance with the strategy's requirements. These come as a result of collaborative learning on the part of the children, and the ability of the teacher to ask the right questions at the right moment so as to require the children to reflect critically and to evaluate their own work. For some teachers this may require a leap of faith to shift the emphasis away from teacher-led instruction to teacher-led learning, a subtle yet crucial shift if LOGO is to be used effectively.

What does LOGO actually do?

Whether a floor or screen turtle is being used, the basic commands and concepts remain the same. The user programs the turtle to move forward a number of 'turtle steps' and to turn through a certain angle, usually expressed as a number of degrees. So, when using a screen turtle, the user might type in 'FORWARD 10', which can be abbreviated to FD 10, and the turtle will move forward 10 turtle steps on the screen. Depending on the program that is being used this could be 10 'generic' steps, or it might be a standard measurement such as millimetres. This is illustrated in Figure 4.1.

Figure 4.1 A simple straight line drawn by a screen turtle

Assuming that the arrowhead represents the turtle, the turtle has moved forward 10 turtle steps from its starting or 'home' position. On the screen version, as the turtle moves forward it leaves a line behind it (see Figure 4.1). Typing 'PEN UP' or 'PU' can disable this feature. This is particularly useful if the user wishes to move the turtle from the completed drawing, or if there is a need to move the turtle to a new part of the drawing without leaving a line. We might now turn the turtle 90 degrees to the right, which would normally follow a command of 'RIGHT 90' ('RT 90') to give the result illustrated by Figure 4.2.

Figure 4.2 The line with the turtle rotated through 90 degrees to the right. The point of the arrow is actually touching the line and therefore indicating a 90 degree turn.

So we now have the commands:

FORWARD 10
RIGHT 90

We can now further extend this concept by completing a square (see Figure 4.3).

Which commands would you use to draw this?

Figure 4.3 A square.

This would be created in the first instance by typing the following commands:

FORWARD 10
RIGHT 90
FORWARD 10
RIGHT 90
FORWARD 10
RIGHT 90
FORWARD 10
RIGHT 90
HIDE TURTLE (this hides the turtle so that it cannot be seen on the screen).

As children progress through the hierarchy of LOGO, they would develop ways of producing the same result with fewer commands. So, for example, if they were using a floor turtle, they could begin by typing in all of the commands separately, as we have done above. The turtle would then obey each command one after the other. So, to begin with the children could enter the commands:

FORWARD 10
RIGHT 90

The turtle would then move forward 10 turtle steps and turns 90 degrees to the right. The next step would be to type in each command four times in the 'correct' order. When so commanded, the turtle would execute all of these commands on the press of one button.

The next extension of this concept would be to use a short command to produce a longer outcome, by the use of repeat commands, such as the one below:

REPEAT 4
FORWARD 10
RIGHT 90
END

Depending upon which type of turtle or LOGO package is being used, this should draw a square. Alternatively, this might be expressed as a formula, thus giving children an early introduction into algebra, for example:

R4 [FD 10, RT 90]
GO

The above statement would make a Roamer Turtle move in a square with each side being 10 turtle steps, which represents a distance of three metres.

We will examine the place and role of LOGO throughout the primary phase, starting with simple LOGO work that can take place in the Foundation stage, through to complex operations that can be completed in Year 6 by using LOGO and control technology packages. This of course is a general progression; there is considerable overlap between these different stages depending on the age and ability of the children and their previous experiences. For example, although a Roamer might be considered a Key Stage 1 tool, the authors have used this successfully with children across the entire primary age range, as indeed we have used the computer turtle with younger children. Illustrated in Figures 4.4 to 4.9 are examples of turtle graphics that the pupils of one of the authors' classes produced with a floor turtle that was controlled directly by the computer. Here a group of Year 4 and 5 children produced drawings using a floor turtle that was controlled by the computer, and then they painted the pictures to make them more colourful and representative of their work.

Figure 4.4 Children sponge painting a picture drawn by the floor turtle.

Figure 4.5 The finished picture.

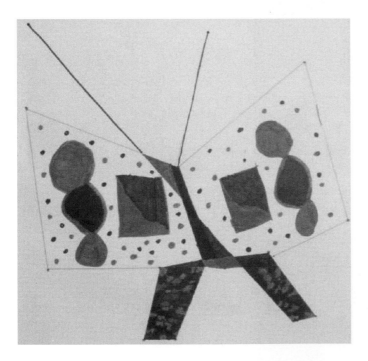

Figure 4.6 A butterfly drawn by the floor turtle and coloured in with felt tip pens.

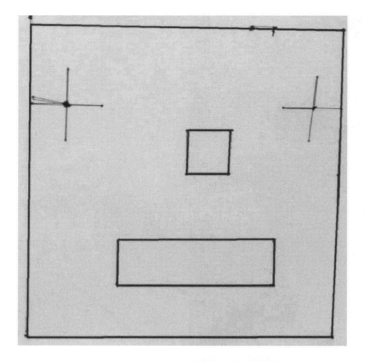

Figure 4.7 A face drawn by the floor turtle.

Figure 4.8 A cabin cruiser drawn by the floor turtle and painted by the children.

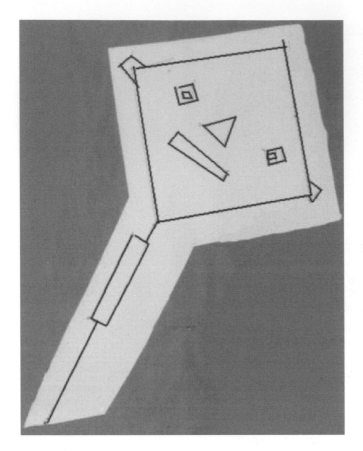

Figure 4.9 A kite.

Using the Roamer, or floor turtle

What is it?

As already described, the Roamer is a programmable toy that allows the user to make it perform a series of movements on the floor. This can take the form of direct commands, where a command is entered and immediately executed, or it might involve a string of commands being entered in sequence. These are subsequently executed when the sequence is complete. For example, the Valiant Roamer, illustrated in Figures 4.10 and 4.11, has a memory that allows it to hold up to 20 separate commands at any one time. This is achieved through the use of a series of large buttons on the top of the device.

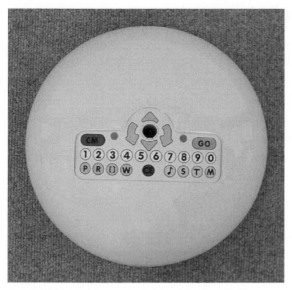

Figure 4.10 A plan view of a Valiant Roamer turtle.

Figure 4.11 A side view of a Valiant Roamer turtle.

Before entering a fresh command or sequence of commands, the user must ensure that the Roamer's memory is cleared of previous commands, otherwise it will execute these existing commands that are already stored before executing any newer ones. This, of course, can cause serious problems, especially with younger users, as it can leave the children with misconceptions as to how the Roamer works and what it can actually do. Pushing the red button marked 'CM', or 'Clear Memory', twice will delete old commands. The children can then enter any new commands and execute them without the new commands being corrupted by any previous instructions that are stored in the memory.

Introducing the floor turtle or Roamer

Before commencing activities based upon the use of a Roamer, Pip or Pixie, the teacher needs to realise that the main emphasis of the first part of the project should be on letting the children explore the model itself, rather than actually telling them how to use it. This in itself may require some modification of teaching style, in that the manner of questioning becomes very important. In order for the children to learn most effectively, it is necessary for the teacher to ask questions that are open-ended in nature. Therefore initial questions to a group of younger children might go something like this:

- ■ 'How do you think we could make the turtle wake up?'
- ■ 'How do you think we could make it move forward?'
- ■ 'How do you think we could make it change direction?'

A fundamental concept of the use of either a floor or screen turtle is that the children must make their own decisions, enter the commands that they think are correct and then evaluate the outcomes. They then have to engage in a process that Papert terms 'debugging', where the user evaluates and reflects upon the processes that achieved that particular outcome and correct it if necessary. This means talking about where they think they might have gone wrong or, if nothing is wrong, how to advance to the next stage. As so much learning actually takes place when errors are made and have to be corrected, we almost welcome the chance to decide how to put such 'errors', i.e. wrong commands, right! This has fundamental implications for teachers. Their role necessarily changes from that of teacher to facilitator, as they need to recognise the learning situations that are developing in front of them and adapt their teaching techniques appropriately and intuitively. It is also important that both teacher and child recognise these stages not as mistakes or errors, but as an essential part of the learning process, stages that they have to go through in order to carry out meaningful tasks. This kind of approach might engender the following questions:

- ■ 'Why do you think the turtle did that?'
- ■ 'What do you think you will have to do to make it do what you wanted it to do?'

The first activity to complete with children in the Foundation Stage might be a simple exercise in getting the children used to how far the device moves in one turtle step. This varies from one device to another, but the Valiant Turtle moves its own diameter, or 30 centimetres, in one step (it can also be programmed to operate in centimetre steps, particularly useful for older children). This might involve asking the children to move it from a start point to a finish point.

Questions might involve:
- 'How many turtle steps will make it stop under that chair?'

This begins to develop an understanding of what a turtle step is, as well as the more focussed mathematical skill of estimation. The children can then think about how far it needs to move. If the children underestimate the distance, then the teacher might ask:
- 'How many more turtle steps are needed?'

Or, if they overestimate the distance:
- 'How many turtle steps too far has it gone?'

This can also be approached from the opposite end, such as:
- 'If I want the turtle to move five turtle steps, where do you think it will stop?'

The children could be given a marker to indicate on the floor where they think it will stop.

A further development of this initial stage would be to ask the children to move the turtle around a simple route that is laid out on the floor. This might involve a play mat with a road map on it, or something simpler such as a series of islands or locations that the turtle has to visit in turn. The exercise immediately introduces the need to turn the turtle a set distance, usually in degrees. This can instantly cause conceptual problems with younger children, who can find using degrees as a measurement a difficult concept. They are used to working with numbers up to 10 or 20, but they find that they have to work with much larger numbers in order to make the floor turtle turn a significant distance (the turtle can be programmed to turn in quarter and half turns, but this, although fine for set figures such as squares, drastically reduces its flexibility). One of the most interesting and challenging elements of the turtle is that to turn it 90 degrees you actually have to tell it this. If you just ask it to turn left or right it will only turn a barely noticeable one degree. Consequently, the children have to discover a way round this, which may require a separate lesson about angles. Most teachers will have realised they can do this by the practical common-sense way of asking children to stand and turn left or right or about turn, and so on. With reference to the corners of the room and other obvious right angles present in the classroom, the authors have found that even children at Key Stage 1 have little difficulty in grasping the concept of a right angle. Once this is understood, the idea of a degree as just another form of measurement, and a right angle having 90 of them, is a reasonable next step. We would hesitate to continue further than this at Key Stage 1 (excepting perhaps 180 and 360 degrees), for that is all that is required at this stage. However, it is a very sound basis for later work, with or without a turtle or, indeed, a computer.

Let us suppose that the children have not yet had to face this problem so that at this stage a typical discussion amongst a group of children using a turtle to visit different locations might look like this:

Teacher: *How far will we need to turn it to make it face the other direction?* (indicating with hands)

Child 1: *One.*

Teacher: *Type that in then.*

Child 1 presses 'CM', then the appropriate direction button, the number '1' button and then 'Go'. The Roamer appears not to move at all.

Teacher: *That wasn't very much was it? Let's have another go. Somebody suggest another number.*

Child 2: *Two.*

Teacher: *Type that in then.*

Child presses 'CM', then the appropriate direction button, the number '2' button and then 'GO'. Again the Roamer appears not to move at all.

As previously mentioned, it takes a little while before the children appreciate that one turtle step will move it a significant distance, but one degree of a turn is barely discernible. However, the children will eventually understand this and when encouraged to count in fives or tens, they quickly appreciate the first concepts of angles, bearings and degrees. This is perhaps the appropriate time for the lesson described above to take place. If similar work about angles has already been covered, then perhaps a little reinforcement may be necessary. This will do no harm: it will be in the context of an enjoyable activity, and need not be boringly repetitive. This is where LOGO is so powerful. It is highly unlikely that these relatively advanced concepts, and this kind of mathematical language, could possibly be taught to such young children without access to a floor turtle. Prior to the advent of the turtle, most children would have been at least a couple of years older before attempting to do any work of this nature. Even with these older children, lessons would probably have had to begin with the limited idea that 90 degrees is a right angle, and other angles would have to wait. Certainly older children would be able to make a right-angled measuring device by drawing a circle, cutting it out, folding it into quarters and then using it to find out whether objects or angles drawn on a worksheet were larger or smaller than a right angle. Although this remains an important mathematical skill that needs to be taught, the whole process can begin much earlier as the children can now access higher levels of mathematical knowledge, skill and understanding much sooner in their school lives.

The next (turtle) steps

Once the children have a basic conceptual awareness of how the turtle works, and of how far a turtle step is, they are then in a position to use this information to produce increasingly complex operations. The Valiant Roamer comes with a very helpful manual and a booklet of ideas for use with children. Additionally, a series of colourful and progressively graded work cards can be purchased. Starting from a series of simple instructions for navigating an obstacle course, the children can progress to producing pictures involving regular shapes, such as houses or boats. This can lead onto work drawing regular polygons with 3, 4, 5, 6 or 7 sides. It is by using such activities as these that the floor turtle can actively develop a range of higher-order concepts. Maps and plans can be drawn. Distances can be estimated, and quarter, half and full turns can be easily understood. The introduction of directional language such as left and right can be developed into work involving the points of the compass. Other projects might include such unlikely activities as writing! Here is an example:
■ 'What letter do these commands make?'

FORWARD 4
BACK 2
RIGHT QUARTER TURN
FORWARD 1
RIGHT QUARTER TURN
FORWARD 2

Assuming that the turtle is pointing in the correct direction to begin with, and that everybody is looking at it from the same perspective, the lower-case letter 'h' should be drawn. (As an aside, it is important to get agreement as to which is the front and back of the turtle before drawing begins, especially where a floor turtle is being used which looks similar regardless of the direction of travel. Children often decorate turtles themselves, using stickers and materials, and some schools buy special covers with faces on them that fit over the turtles.) Conversely, the teacher might give the pupils specific letters of the alphabet and then get them to draw the letter.
■ 'Which commands would I need to draw the letter E as a capital?'

This of course would depend upon the starting position, and how the children had been taught to write capital letters. Capitals work better, but examples such as the above, where there are plenty of straight lines and quarter turns, can be used. This will be particularly relevant if the activity is carried out with younger children. It should be noted at this point that floor turtles are not particularly good at drawing circles or any kind of curved lines. They are often slightly inaccurate at the best of times, often depending on the floor surface that is being used, and any error is compounded when drawing a circle.

However, let us think about the mathematics involved. We want the children to understand the concepts needed to draw a circle. Given that a complete turn is composed of 360 degrees, any circle has to involve at least 10 lots of 36, or 10×36, or 36×10, as well as having some forward movement in order to actually draw the circle (otherwise it would simply pivot on the spot). The whole point of using LOGO is to get the children to understand the properties of how shapes are drawn through programming the correct sequence of commands. Quite complex mathematics can be achieved in this way with older children, but as we have described above, there is plenty of scope for the younger user.

What if I don't have a floor turtle?

Don't despair! Children can be utilised as the floor turtles themselves. Indeed, the authors used to play games to practise directional skills with even Year 5 and 6 children, even when they had full access to a floor turtle and several LOGO programs on a computer. These games introduce and reinforce the basic concepts that are necessary before using any LOGO turtle – the notion of left and right, forward and backward, and the importance of facing the right way at the start. With the youngest children this might involve taking them into the hall or onto the playground and getting them all to face in the same direction (not towards the teacher as they will then all be facing in different directions, depending on where they are standing in relation to the teacher). Facing the wall of the school will do very well. The lesson may develop with the following instructions:

- 'Put your left hand in the air.'
- 'Put your right hand in the air.'
- 'Turn a quarter turn to the right.'
- 'Turn a quarter turn to the left.'
- 'Turn a half turn to the right.'
- 'Turn a half turn to the left.'

The next stage will involve movement:
- ■ 'Move one (turtle) step forward.'
- ■ 'Move one (turtle) step backward.'

And then start to put sequences of movement together:
- ■ 'Move forward one step.'
- ■ 'Turn a quarter turn to the right.'
- ■ 'Move forward one step.'

This can then be developed to include quite complex sequences of instructions. It enables the children to appreciate the importance of using the correct syntax (perhaps by using the traditional game Simon Says), for as we have already discovered, if the exact commands are not used the turtle will not work. It develops the children's listening and sequencing skills, and requires them to concentrate. This activity can be extended in a number of ways. The children can be asked to work in pairs and be given instructions to get round an obstacle, or the earlier example of giving instructions to make a letter or shape could also be productively employed in that one child can be asked to give instructions to the other. These can be written down at the time, so that later they can decide if they had chosen the correct sequence. Alternatively, as an extension activity, or when using these activities with older children, the phrases 'quarter turn' or 'half turn' can be replaced by specific angles, such as 90, 180 or 270 degrees.

Asking children to write instructions so that another can later follow them is an illuminating experience. Try it with simple construction kits. Ask one child to make up a simple toy, such as a basic aeroplane shape – body, wings and a tail. Ask them next to write the instructions for making this same model so that another child, by following these instructions, can replicate it. The words should be simple, such as 'thin long piece' or 'short white block'. It will also be very important that the instructions should be in the correct sequence. Teachers should try this out first, and be warned, it is not as easy as it sounds. It is fascinating to see, without practice, what strange shapes can materialise.

Once the children have understood the importance of having the correct orientation before beginning any type of turtle graphics, the degrees of a circle can be introduced. This would include the concept of 90 degrees equalling a quarter turn, 180 degrees equalling a half turn and so on. Plenty of this work could be done away from the computer, and could then be extended into the properties of individual shapes, such as a square.

When the children have understood the concept of the turtle, and have had a go at being a human turtle, they should be able to make a direct connection between the way that they move and the way that the turtle moves. However, they will then need to think about how they made the turtle move, or, if they have not yet used it, how it will move. How many of us adults, let alone primary age children, ever analyse to any degree just how we actually move across the floor? We do it automatically, without thinking. Yet the floor turtle can only move when it is programmed to do so by a human. Although it moves through space as we do, albeit in only two dimensions, the children will recognise the need to break every single action down as a separate task or instruction. Therefore, when they make the switch from the concrete experience of a floor or human turtle, to the more abstract screen turtle, they should still be able to appreciate that the screen turtle moves 'forward' rather than 'up'.

Why we use the Roamer or floor turtle?

The use of a floor turtle provides a number of opportunities for developing a wide range of mathematical, language, and wider social and educational skills with children right across the primary phase.

Subject specific skills

Mathematical skills

As one might reasonably expect with a tool of this nature, mathematics is probably the curriculum area that can most benefit from the use of the floor turtle. These skills and ideas can include measurement, including distance, direction, angles and bearings and the points of the compass; shape and space, including regular and irregular shapes; and mental arithmetic, including number bonds and algebra.

The use of a floor turtle can develop children's ability to estimate, a very important mathematical skill. We have already given examples of how this might involve asking children to suggest how many steps it will take the turtle to reach a particular point on the floor (or, later on in time, on a screen). We have also asked how many parts of a turn will be required to have it facing in a certain direction. With older children this can lead to more specific geographical work involving distance, angles and bearings, as well as specific direction-orientated language that includes points of the compass. Other uses can also include work on space and shape through the use of regular polygons. Number bonds can be developed by the use of focused questioning on the part of the teacher, such as

■ 'How many more turtle steps will park the turtle under the chair?'

A further development can lead to some basic algebra work. This might involve the children using the repeat commands to draw a square, which has already been discussed in this chapter. As a general rule, young children will use many commands to make the turtle perform only a few operations, whereas older children will use a few commands to get the turtle to produce many outcomes. Older children should be encouraged to write their own programs within LOGO. These are called procedures and are written to produce more complex outcomes. For example, a square that is repeated many times in a different position to produce a complex geometric shape can be drawn by entering only one command. Admittedly, some programming would be needed to achieve this outcome, but by the end of Key Stage 2 a minimum of key strokes should achieve quite complex outcomes. This applies not only to the screen turtle, but also to the floor turtle.

Language skills

Although not the main focus of this book, these skills are also relevant to mathematics as they are crucial to this type of learning. The landmark report from 1982, *Mathematics Counts*, which is more normally referred to as the Cockcroft Report (DES, 1982) stressed the importance of developing and using correct mathematical language. The use of a floor turtle encourages speaking and listening, sequencing, the formulating and the giving of concise instructions, as well as the need to write, evaluate, edit and even refine these instructions. This is undertaken in the context of collaborative learning and group work. These are skills that should be developed simultaneously. The learning engendered through the use of a floor turtle is most powerful when children are working together. They should work in groups of two or three, as this will engender a free flow of ideas and discussion. Quite apart from developing the social skills described below, the children will need to speak clearly and politely, and listen carefully to the contributions of the other members of the group. Sequencing is critical to the successful operation of any LOGO-driven turtle, for as we have already seen, if the commands are not entered correctly, the response will either be incorrect, or there will be no response at all. This in turn leads to the need for editing skills. Thus, the children will have to read through what has been written or entered as previous commands, identify where the error is and then debug it. This process is revisited until the outcome is exactly as intended. As a natural extension of this, these higher-order reading and analytical skills lead to the children further developing cognitively in a wide range of holistic ways – very much in line with the teachings of both Jean Piaget and Seymour Papert.

General educational skills

Social skills

As implied above, LOGO is an excellent vehicle for the development of a wide range of social skills. All collaborative learning should engender discussion, taking turns, teamwork and co-operation, all of which are very important in any classroom, from the Foundation Stage onwards. This is a principal generic skill, and can be developed especially through the use of LOGO and in particular, by the floor turtle.

Cognitive skills

Spatial awareness

Quite apart from the subject-specific skills that can be developed with the use of the floor turtle, its use also involves very important higher-order learning skills such as the development of spatial awareness, or the ability to think in two dimensions. This is important in that it encourages children to think about the location of different objects or features in relation to one another, and forms the basis for the development of the concepts for understanding maps and plans. This will include an understanding that a plan view is only the top of something when viewed directly from above. This is a very difficult concept for young children to grasp, but by having a bird's eye view of what the turtle is doing, and in fact taking the place of the 'bird' itself, they have a better chance of understanding it. They are also presented with an opportunity to grapple with the mechanics of scale and ratios. A map is a kind of scale drawing, and therefore every point has to be drawn to scale, and be correct in distance-ratio, if not in size, to the real thing.

Logical thinking

Another important generic and higher-order skill is the development of logical thinking. This is a particularly important mathematical skill, in that it enables the child to make reasoned judgements as to the accuracy of a problem. The need to program the floor turtle in a particular way in order to achieve a particular outcome demands not only that the commands are accurately 'written', using the correct language or code, but also that they are in the correct sequence. So, once the children have modelled the situation that they want to develop, and once the commands have been entered, the children need to be able to identify and correct any errors that may occur. We have already mentioned that Papert felt that this 'debugging' is an important part of the learning process, and in using the floor turtle the children are encouraged to develop all the thinking skills that are so necessary to complete the whole learning process.

Conclusion

Once the children are fully conversant with the mechanics of the floor turtle, and are comfortable with its use, they will be able to use it as a basis for development into other areas of LOGO. In the next chapter, we will discuss how the teacher can manage the transition between floor and screen turtles. However, the floor turtle can also act as a launch pad for the development of other areas in the mathematics curriculum. Geometry, co-ordinates and vectors are all areas of mathematics that require diagrams, mapping or plots. In later chapters we shall suggest how these can be done and how such programs as LOGO can both enhance existing areas of the mathematical curriculum and enrich the ICT teaching within the classroom.

Bibliography

Papert, S., *Mindstorms: Children, Computers and Powerful Ideas*, second edition, Harvester Wheatsheaf, London, 1980.
DES, *Mathematics Counts* (The Cockcroft Report), HMSO, London, 1982.

Chapter 5

The transition from floor turtle to screen turtle

Once the children have experienced the use of a floor turtle, or have acted as a 'human turtle', they are ready to progress to using a screen LOGO package. This is a piece of software that runs on a computer, and is based around driving a screen turtle. Some packages can drive both a screen and floor turtle, which is very useful as it enables the children to transfer their learning on the floor directly into the more abstract context of the screen environment. This kind of package was often a common feature in the earlier days of LOGO, as the floor turtles were not technologically advanced enough to operate independently of a computer. This is not the case today of course, but programs such as *Roamer World* do simulate the appearance and movement of the Roamer on the screen. As described later, this helps the children to transfer what they see of the actual movement of the floor turtle to the more abstract concepts required for the screen turtle.

During the previous chapter we discussed the importance of children using a floor turtle, entirely separate from the computer, as part of their first LOGO experiences. Although not essential, this is highly desirable, otherwise the children often find it difficult to transfer their ideas from the 'real' three-dimensional environment to the conceptually more abstract two-dimensional screen turtle. Rather than perceiving the movement of the turtle on the screen as 'forward' or 'backward', children often perceive it as 'up' and 'down', which is clearly an incorrect interpretation of what is actually going on. However, if the children have the opportunity to use a floor turtle, or act as a 'human turtle' then this is less likely to happen. The two main aspects of LOGO can be introduced and used simultaneously. Preliminary activities can involve a floor or 'human' turtle, which can then be reinforced by use of the screen-based LOGO package.

Learning to control the screen turtle

Most modern computer-based LOGO software packages have a range of useful functions that enable the conceptual gap between the 'concrete' real world of the floor turtle and the more abstract environment of the screen turtle to be successfully bridged. These include a series of prepared screens which act as a background, allowing the turtle to be moved around the screen, in the same way that a floor turtle might be moved around on a play mat. This could be a road or some other kind of route. The *2Simple Infant Video Toolbox* contains a program called *2Go*, which is a very basic LOGO type package designed for use by children in the foundation stage. Although an excellent suite of programs for all aspects of the early years curriculum, certain elements of it are particularly useful for children at this early stage of their development. On opening the package the user is presented with a blank screen that has a series of simple direction and distance buttons, which are used to move the turtle around the screen. When the user moves the turtle, it moves in a distinct series of steps that allow the user to compare the distance entered to the amount that the turtle actually moves. This is illustrated in Figure 5.1, where a square with a side of 10 turtle steps has been drawn.

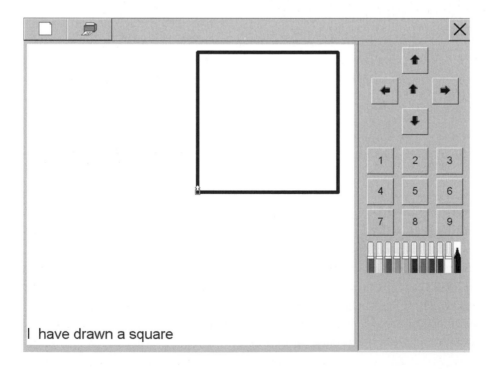

I have drawn a square

Figure 5.1 A square which has been drawn on the LOGO package *2Go*, part of the *2Simple Infant Video Toolbox*.

The software allows the user to write a sentence at the bottom of the screen, as well as to select 11 different colours from the bottom right-hand corner of the screen. These appear as a series of felt tip pens. The white one is particularly useful, as it can also be used as an eraser. It is also very useful when using the prepared backgrounds, which are often coloured. There are several of these, including a racetrack, an island, and a village. Another one of these, a space scene where white is essential, is illustrated in Figure 5.2.

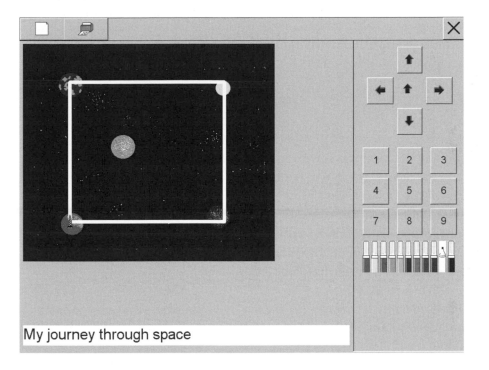

My journey through space

Figure 5.2 A screenshot of the space scene from *2Go*, where the user has visited some of the planets. Again, this is a square of side 10 turtle steps, the same size as the square on the previous illustration.

In the early stages of using the screen turtle, similar activities can be covered as with the floor turtle. By asking the children to replicate on the screen activities that they previously carried out with the floor turtle, the teacher is helping the children to reinforce the connections between the concrete use of the floor turtle and the abstract environment of the screen turtle. The drawing of the square is a good example of this, and similar learning opportunities can be exploited even for older children. For example, the number and arrow buttons provide many opportunities for developing basic numeracy and literacy skills. As previously mentioned, the squares illustrated on the screenshots above are of side 10 turtle steps. Initially, the children might move between the planets one turtle step at a time. However, using skilled intervention from an adult, the children can be encouraged to think in groups of numbers, so they might move in steps of two at a time. This in turn leads to the first steps in the development of multiplication tables. So:

2 STEPS + 2 STEPS +2 STEPS + 2 STEPS + 2 STEPS EQUALS 10 STEPS, or
5 LOTS OF TWO STEPS EQUALS 10 STEPS, or
5 TIMES TWO EQUALS 10.

The opportunity also exists here for some work with number bonds. The children can experiment with different combinations of numbers in order to reach 10, perhaps recording them on the way:

3 STEPS + 2 STEPS + 4 STEPS + 1 STEP EQUALS 10 STEPS.

The teacher might then ask the following questions such as:
- 'How many different ways can you make 10?'
- 'How many more steps will make 10?'
- 'You have gone too far there. How many steps will you need to move backward in order to be in the correct place?'

This might then be developed into other areas, such as geometric shapes, an example of which is illustrated in Figure 5.3.

This can subsequently be developed to extend the children's knowledge and understanding of number bonds. The kind of questions that the teacher might pose include:
- 'How many turtle steps has the turtle gone through altogether?'
- 'How many turtle steps are needed to draw two sides of the square?'
- 'How many more turtle steps are needed to go all of the way round the square?'

By working in multiples of 10, the children's knowledge and understanding of number bonds and counting in 10s can be developed. One of the main advantages of LOGO is the ability to develop several key mathematical skills at once. So, just by working through the three basic activities illustrated above, the children have covered the following key mathematical areas:
- Counting in 10s
- Number bonds
- Counting on
- Introduction to tables
- Introduction to right angles.

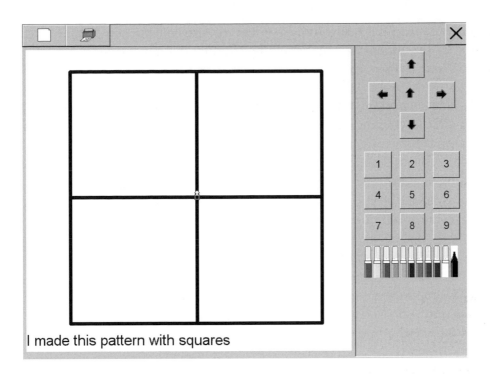

I made this pattern with squares

Figure 5.3 Four squares of side 10 turtle steps used to make a geometric pattern.

And, in the wider educational sense:
■ Collaborative learning
■ Working with other people
■ Spatial awareness.

Once the children have an initial understanding of the basic concepts of LOGO, they can move onto more complex activities. If suitable programs are available, by the time the children have completed the Reception Year, they should be able to control the movement of a basic turtle around both screen and floor. They should then be encouraged to use degrees to gain a finer control of the angles. For many children, it may not be a sufficient challenge just to move a screen turtle through a quarter turn (or 90 degrees at a time). The children will very quickly become bored with the inflexibility of this program, especially if they have already managed to turn a floor turtle a given number of degrees to move it in a specific direction.

The children will now be in a position to produce more accurate drawings with the screen turtle than was possible with the floor turtle, although there may need to be some considerable exploratory work undertaken on their part. They will need to develop an instinctive idea of how many degrees produce a certain amount of turn from the turtle. Indeed, in the earliest stages it may be necessary for the teacher to actually tell the children that 90 degrees is a right angle, or 'square corner'. This has been discussed in Chapter 4 .

However, this conceptual development is exactly what LOGO is designed to engender. A LOGO package such as *Imagine Logo* from Logotron is ideal for this. As with *2Go*, the software allows the turtle to be moved over a prepared background, but also has greater flexibility in that it allows the turtle to be turned through any number of given degrees and this can be achieved in several different ways. One of the most versatile LOGO packages on the market, *Imagine Logo* has several level options, including a simple point and click turtle LOGO (illustrated in Figure 5.4), a more comprehensive LOGO program for older pupils and a multimedia authoring program, allowing presentations and animations to be made using LOGO commands. This package allows the simple LOGO concept, as originally envisaged by Papert, to be extended in a number of interesting and exciting ways that are wholly appropriate for teaching mathematics with ICT at the beginning of the twenty-first century.

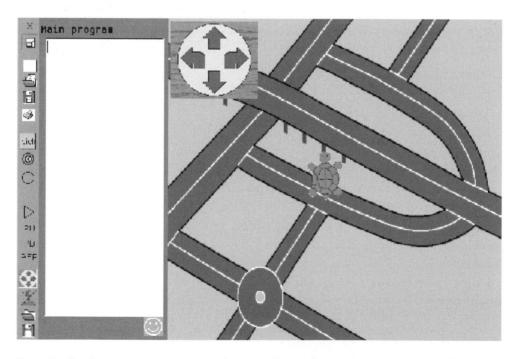

Figure 5.4 The *Simple Turtle* screen option, which is part of the *Imagine Logo* package from Logotron. The toolbox enables the user to point and click to enter instructions. The forward and back arrows move the turtle, and the left and right arrows turn it. This is then recorded on the left-hand side of the screen, and can be edited in the same way that one might edit a piece of word processed text. The turtle's position changes accordingly.

Figure 5.7 illustrates a screen where the turtle has been moved around the road network, returning to the original starting point, leaving a line, or trail. At the start, the pen was raised so that the turtle could be moved from the original starting position in the middle of the screen to a convenient starting point without leaving a trail. Then the pen was lowered to leave a trail, and then it was moved around the roads by means of clicking on the appropriate commands on the screen. This is illustrated by Figure 5.5.

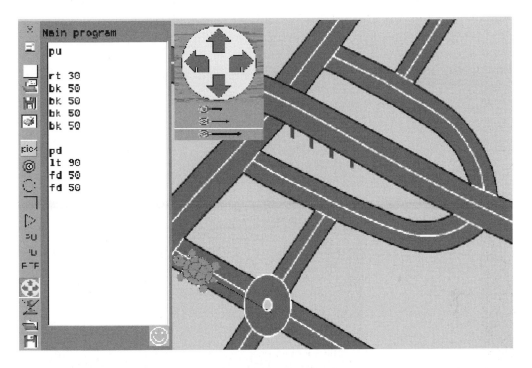

Figure 5.5 The turtle is moved to a new starting position. When selecting the direction of travel, a small drop-down menu appears to allow the user to select the required distance. Each of the options allows the turtle to move 10, 20 and 50 turtle steps respectively.

The commands for this are:

PENUP	Raised the pen;
RIGHT 30	Turned the turtle through 30 degrees to the right;
BACK 50	Moved it backward 50 turtle steps. This was repeated a further three times to move it onto the roundabout;
PENDOWN	Lowered the pen so that a trail was left when it was moved;
LEFT 90	Turned the turtle in the required direction of travel;
FORWARD 50	Moved the turtle forward 50 turtle steps;
FORWARD 50	Moved it forward another 20 turtle steps.

At this point the teacher can ask questions that extend the children's learning and thinking skills such as 'How many steps has the turtle moved in total?' The children can get this information either from their memories of using number bonds or mental arithmetic, or from using the record that the program has produced for them.

The turtle then has to be turned 100 degrees to the right in order to get it to face in the correct direction. This is where the next possible error and misconception might appear, for the initial reaction might be to turn it only 80 degrees, which is effectively the 'inside angle' of the turn. This is illustrated by Figure 5.6.

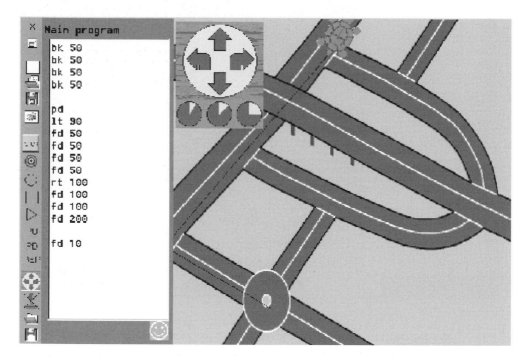

Figure 5.6 The turtle is turned through 100 degrees to the right. It is important to appreciate that the 'outside' angle is required, not the 'inside' angle which would be 80 degrees. When the left or right buttons are selected, three simple options appear which when clicked turn the turtle 30, 45 or 90 degrees respectively.

Again, opportunities suddenly exist for the teacher to encourage the development of a whole host of numeracy-related concepts, skills and understanding. These might include:

■ 'Why do you think that you have had to turn the turtle so far?'

The turtle then moves around the road network until it is back at the starting point. This is illustrated by Figure 5.7.

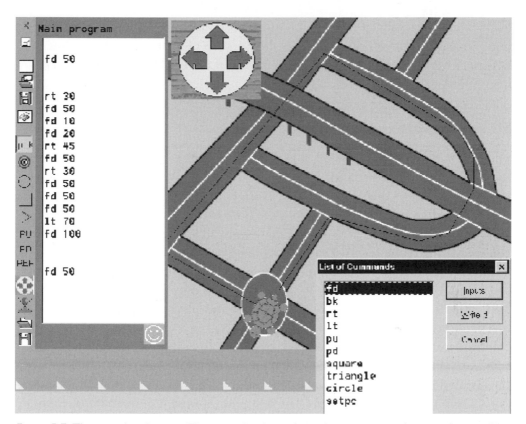

Figure 5.7 The completed route. The route has been drawn by a screen turtle, using *Imagine Logo* from Logotron. The commands on the left can be entered via the turtle toolbox (the arrows at the top of the screen), by clicking on *pick* from the menu on the left-hand side and selecting the required command from the list (the box at the bottom of the screen), or by typing the commands directly into the pane on the left-hand side of the screen. These commands can then subsequently be edited or 'debugged' if they are incorrect, or do not produce the desired outcome.

The teacher might then ask the children to calculate the distance that the turtle has travelled in total, or along a particular leg. The children can then look at the commands that have been entered into the pane in order to produce the movements from the turtle. These can then be reviewed, refined and edited. This is a very valuable exercise, as it enables the children to get into the habit of writing programs (for that is what they are) in a concise and accurate form. These very important skills will be required in the later stages of LOGO as it enables the children to fit more commands into a given space. It also enables the children to develop their awareness of number bonds and number skills. For example, where there are two consecutive commands of FORWARD 20, these can be refined to one command of FORWARD 40. Where a LEFT 90 is followed immediately by a RIGHT 5, this can be rewritten as LEFT 85. It also enables the children to get a 'feel' for the program in the sense that they will very quickly develop an awareness of how far the turtle needs to be turned or moved in order to get the desired outcome. It is this process of refinement and debugging that Papert felt was crucial to the whole point of using LOGO, and encourages the children to 'think LOGO'.

More complex drawings

The next step in the progression of LOGO will be for the children to produce drawings using regular shapes, such as houses or cars. When using the screen turtle it is desirable to ensure that they work with increasing accuracy, especially when using angles. As with the floor turtle, it is also crucial to ensure that they are working in pairs so that there is a collaborative effort, in that both children are working together to produce one, common outcome. Effort is balanced, and the input of both members is of equal value to the outcome. The discussion that the pairs engage in is crucial to the development of their individual learning and the understanding of the LOGO package as a whole. It is very tempting for the teacher to jump in at this point and give the answer to the children, but this needs to be resisted as much as possible. The teacher needs to take a step back and listen to the quality of the discourse between the users, and thus be in a position to steer the discussion in the right direction, without giving the answer away. It is the process that is important here, not the outcome. After all, as we have already made clear, the finished drawings at this stage will not be great art. If that is what is required, as far as it is possible to compute art at all, then an art or graphics package should be used. The authors have used both, and the relevance to mathematics are discussed in a later chapter.

It is at this point in the process that the teacher needs to make a decision about how more difficult shapes should be tackled, especially circles. As we discussed in the previous chapter, this can prove to be difficult. The children may want to produce cars, but the circles needed for the wheels are difficult to 'draw' freehand using the commands entered by the children due to the mathematical nature of the commands required to produce them. Each circle will be made up of many little straight lines that may not even complete the circle. *First Logo* has the advantage in that it has an option that enables a circle to be drawn without individual commands. This can be edited to produce circles of different diameters. However, in a sense this is contrary to the underlying philosophy of LOGO, which is to encourage the users to define their own programs and requirements. How far this philosophy can be taken will depend on several key issues. The age and ability of the children is the main factor, but the flexibility of the program that is being used may well be another. Nevertheless, there will be instances when the children may need to produce circles to enhance their own work. It is also a valuable exercise in writing commands within a program. In order to draw a circle, LOGO needs the essential information on the products that compose a circle. So, for example, the turtle would need to move forward at least one step, and then turn through a number of degrees which is a property of 360 (as 360 degrees are needed to construct a circle). Therefore, a command might ask the turtle to move forward one step and turn 10 degrees 36 times. The size of the circle can be adjusted by changing the angle of turn, or the number of steps that the turtle moves in one go, but whatever happens, both turn and distance must be consistent and the final total of turn must always equal 360.

Control technology

Although this area of the curriculum might appear to be a long way from mathematics, control technology provides a logical conclusion to LOGO, particularly the concept of 'programming' the computer to achieve an intended outcome. The work that we have described above, and in the previous chapter, is a precursor to the understanding of control programs. It is not the purpose of this book to describe all the factors involved in control technology. Although apparently one of the least taught areas of the primary curriculum (see many OFSTED [Office of Standards in Education] reports), it can be one of the most rewarding. Whether the model to be controlled by the computer is one that has been made by the children themselves, or if it is one in kit form, the 'peripheral learning' that can take place is considerable. By peripheral we do not only mean the construction of the model as a design project, as important as this is. Nor do we mean the necessary knowledge of science that may be required to understand the workings of the mechanics and electronics that may be part of the model. For the purposes of this book we are particularly concerned with the mathematical processes involved in making a suitable program to work the model.

As suggested above, there are two basic technological approaches that can be followed in the teaching of control technology. Children can make their own models in the classroom, and then learn to control it by writing their own instructions, and enter them into a computer using a suitable program, such as *CoCo* from Commotion. The second method is to use a ready-made model together with software such as *Robolab*, which can be used with the *Lego Mindstorms* equipment. The programs exhibit a range of clear icons, and all that is required is for the children to decide what they want the model to do, and click on the relevant icons. This is obviously a much simpler and less time-consuming approach than having the children make their own model first and program it themselves. However, as the mathematics involved is largely connected with the writing of programs, this should perhaps be an inherent part of all control technology, for it asks the children what they want their model to do, and to think clearly what commands – their instructions to the computer – they should use. This can easily be done even when using the kit form of control. The children still need to decide what the model should do, and sequence the icons accordingly. If at the same time they are asked to explain exactly (as far as possible) what they think happens when the icon is activated, i.e. what command is given to the computer, then the process is very similar for both control systems. The authors are not suggesting that there must always be a massive pen-and-paper introduction to this activity. However, in our experience children enjoy finding out how things work, and when so motivated, are happy to record what they discover or hope to discover. Indeed, by thinking about what will happen, and writing out a program to help them understand what is going on, we have found that children are more likely to enjoy the subsequent practical work.

Writing a program

If we take the first of the control processes described above, children need to write a list of commands, and the actual language of these commands is governed by the type and make of program used. The model to be controlled may include lights, motors and various switches, so a program, using typical command words may look like this:

REPEAT FOREVER (In fact as long as you want, and until you command it to stop.)
WAIT UNTIL INPUT 1 IS OFF (This would be a switch of some kind, a light cell or a pressure pad.)
SWITCH ON 1 (This could be a light or a buzzer.)
WAIT 3. (It will be on for three seconds.)
SWITCH OFF 1 (The light or buzzer is switched off.)
WAIT 3 (No light or buzzer for this length of time. Another SWITCH ON 1 command will re-activate it.)
MOTOR D ON (Motors are connected to two outputs, so that it can be given the commands FORWARD or BACKWARD if necessary – in this case it doesn't matter.)
WAIT 5
END REPEAT (Combines with the repeat command, which shows commands to be repeated.)
END PROCEDURE (Ends the complete sequence of commands.)

This program describes a relatively simple series of commands, although there can be a limit to how many lines – often only 20 – that can be used. However, if children have had plenty of experience with floor and screen turtles, they will soon understand how to circumvent this by learning to include various procedures, which are in essence programs within programs.

Children, with the guidance of their teacher, would only write their finished programs after they had first decided how their model should perform. They might at this stage jot down their ideas in note form, or perhaps see if they could describe it in the form of a flowchart.

Flowcharts

These can be used to plan any activity from making bread to constructing a car, or running a school or even a large company. However, they are often associated with computers because they are used as an aid to designing programs. They are important during the planning stage of any activity that needs to be programmed, and may be used to highlight any possible problems that might occur during the preparation for analysis by a computer. As the digital computer is based on binary notation, a flowchart must ask questions which only require a yes or no answer. There is nothing mysterious or even particularly difficult in writing a flowchart. However, it is important to decide when they are relevant. Figure 5.8 (overleaf) shows an example of a flowchart which could easily be planned and written by children. It would be a valuable teaching and learning experience if more children were encouraged to plan any activity in this way. An ideal use for the interactive whiteboard, perhaps? However, if we look at the program designed for the working model above, is there any advantage in first writing it out as a flowchart? The program as written above is a step-by-step sequence of instructions. The flowcharts in Figures 5.8 and 5.9 overleaf, simple though they might be, require the reader (human or computer) to make decisions, and act upon these decisions. The control program detailed above has already made these decisions, although during the planning stage, if yes or no questions needed to be asked, perhaps a flowchart would have been useful.

Boolean Algebra

Named after the mathematician George Boole (1815–64), Boolean Algebra is based on the simple premise that every action can be determined by breaking it down into a series yes or no decisions. Try it and see: choose a simple activity such as opening a bottle and find out just how many stages are needed with yes or no answers. You might even write a flowchart.

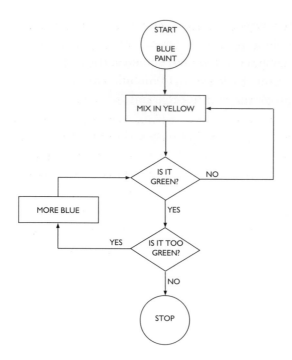

Figure 5.8 A simple flowchart to illustrate mixing paints.

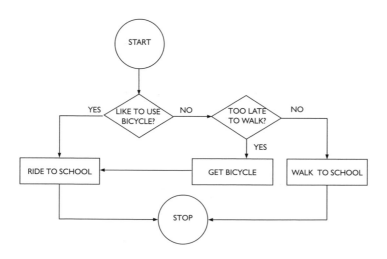

Figure 5.9 A simple flowchart to illustrate travelling to school. Note the different shaped question boxes and the yes/no loops. The flowchart itself can be one large loop.

Boolean logic has subsequently been applied to the area of mathematics that includes much of the work on sets, Venn diagrams, and 'switching functions'. The first two should be familiar to all primary teachers, but they may not perhaps have met 'switches', or not at least as a mathematical concept. Obviously much of this work is beyond the scope of the primary school mathematics curriculum. However, as the diagrams in Figures 5.10 to 5.13 show, there are areas of this work that could quite easily be done by older Key Stage 2 children. These examples require on or off, yes or no answers; whether they make their decision based on general knowledge or in a practical science lesson, these examples illustrate not only simple circuitry, but also help to show how digital computers work. These computers can be thought of as a countless series of switches, which may always be on (yes) or off (no). It is the binary nature of these computers that gave rise to the application of Boolean logic to various

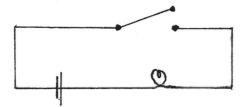

Figure 5.10 'Standard' one bulb, one switch circuit.

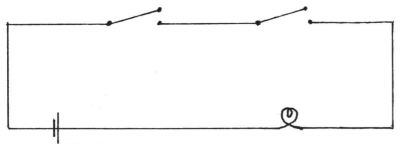

Figure 5.11 When both switches are closed then light is on.

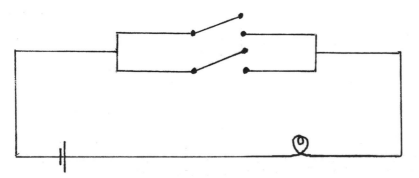

Figure 5.12 When one switch is closed then light is on.

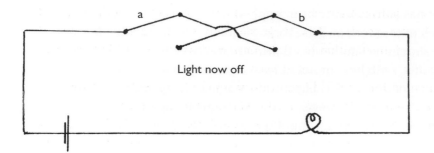

Figure 5.13 Cross-over switch? (Think of it as a kind of double number 2 type circuit.) Only one switch (a or b) has to 'move' for the light to be on.

aspects of electronics, in a similar way that this thinking can be applied to classification and the use of sets.

A turtle case study

Our thanks to Karen Smith, who is currently at Kenningtons Primary School, Aveley, Thurrock, for this description of her work with children at her previous schools. On both occasions the work was carried out with a mixed class from Years 4 and 5.

As some of the children in this case study had not worked with the 'turtle' before, the first lesson was spent introducing it. For those who had used it, the lesson was a useful and pleasant form of revision. Working in small groups they programmed the floor turtle to complete simple sequences, as well as working in pairs to guide each other round the playground using basic commands such as 'one', meaning one step. In this way they became used to the idea of using such commands for the turtle.

In another but concurrent lesson, the children drew treasure maps on 2 cm squared paper. As well as the treasure, the children marked in mountains, swamps and quicksands. They marked the start position for the turtle, and then wrote their own instructions, so that the turtle could avoid the obstacles and find the treasure. For this each square represented 1 – hence 'FORWARD 3' meant forward three squares.

The exercise was first tried out using the floor turtle. However, as soon as the children were happy and confident using this they were introduced to the screen version. They observed the direction that the screen turtle was facing, and then how it moved. They experimented with the 'PEN UP' and 'PEN DOWN' commands, and discovered that they could choose the colour and thickness of the lines drawn on the screen. Working in small groups in the school's computer suite, the children typed in simple instructions and watched the turtle move.

Once all of the children had had this opportunity to 'play' with the program, they were able to type in simple instructions for drawing a square. They compared squares drawn using commands 'FORWARD 4' and 'FORWARD 100'. They also compared these with similar commands given to the floor turtle, as the screen turtle steps are smaller than those of the floor version.

The children were then given a simple set of instructions, e.g.:

FORWARD 4
RIGHT 90
FORWARD 4
RIGHT 90
FORWARD 4
RIGHT 90
FORWARD 4
RIGHT 90

The children were then asked to predict the shape that these commands would make on the screen. Back in the classroom, the children drew their initials on squared paper, and then together with a partner worked out a set of instructions so that their initials could be replicated on the screen. These were later printed out, much to the children's delight.

Later on in the term, the children were introduced to the 'REPEAT' command, and were given instructions such as:

REPEAT 4 (FORWARD 100, LEFT 90).
REPEAT 3 (FORWARD 150, RIGHT 120).
REPEAT 6 (FORWARD 100, RIGHT 60).

After discussing what they thought the shapes might be, they then entered the commands into the screen turtle to see if they were correct.

Finally the children created their own mathematical patterns similar to those that could be created using the 'Spirograph' drawing kit. The children used the repeat command to enter much larger numbers – 'REPEAT 25' – and experimented with different angles – 'REPEAT 25 (FORWARD 100, RIGHT 75).

They watched the different shapes that these commands produced. By this time they were able to make their own suggestions for different programs and commands, such as the numbers of steps or repeats. The resulting patterns were later displayed in the classroom.

Many teachers will have recognised that some of this work follows that suggested by the QCA 'Unit 4E: Modelling Effects on Screen'. However, this is a real-life example of how this work can be done, in two different schools with different classes of children. Although based on the QCA scheme, much of the project came from the teacher's own planning. It was necessary to decide just what part of the scheme was suitable for these particular children, and when and if other work should be included. The work in the playground, the stages between the floor and screen turtles and the final pattern drawings were just such examples.

Obviously some of the children found the work more difficult than others. Nevertheless, all were able to accomplish as much as they were able and, with the minimum of help (one very competent learning support assistant for some of the time in one school), the majority completed the entire project.

Karen Smith has also used *Roamer World* with children in the Reception class, albeit with one-to-one support. They managed very well to guide an object round the screen. They particularly enjoyed the space program with the rocket and planets.

Conclusion

This chapter has described the logical progression from the floor turtle to the screen turtle, and in particular the progression from the concrete to the abstract. This has included the peripheral activities associated with these, such as designing flowcharts and the use of Boolean algebra.

Chapter 6

Why does LOGO merit a place in the primary mathematics curriculum?

In our roles as teacher trainers, we are often asked by trainees, 'What is the point of LOGO, and what exactly does it do? In an already overcrowded curriculum, and especially a maths curriculum, why should we bother with it?' Quite apart from the fact that it is one of the few specific applications that is mentioned in the National Curriculum ICT document (DfEE/QCA, 1999), the purpose of this chapter is to answer these important questions. The previous two chapters have suggested how LOGO can be delivered across the primary phase through the use of screen and floor turtles, and control technology. This chapter discusses and then summarises the overall contribution that the use of LOGO tools can bring to the primary curriculum, both in terms of mathematics and the wider, generic primary school learning skills. It will also attempt to discuss the role of the teacher in ensuring that the children come to 'think LOGO' in an appropriate way.

Due to the open-ended nature of LOGO, and the largely process-orientated and investigative approach to learning that it engenders, there are clear implications for the role of both the teacher and the child. If LOGO is to be delivered in line with Papert's original philosophy as mentioned in his book *Mindstorms* (1980), then the teacher has a definite role to perform as an educator, and the child has a clear role to perform as a learner. This is quite a sophisticated relationship that operates at many different levels, and will be explored below.

Why use LOGO?

We have already discussed in the previous chapters the particular skills and concepts that are influenced by LOGO within the primary mathematics curriculum and beyond. The skills that are developed through the use of LOGO can be directly transferred to other areas of mathematics, as well as other areas of the primary curriculum. The problem-solving and investigative approach that form the basis of the philosophy of LOGO can be directly applied within a whole range of mathematical contexts, whether ICT is used or not. This approach is also particularly relevant to those obviously practical subjects such as science, geography and technology.

Although we have already discussed and explained the key contributions that LOGO can make to teaching and learning in previous chapters, we make no apology for mentioning them again here. We believe strongly that LOGO is one of the few ICT applications available to the primary teacher that genuinely provides an open-ended learning environment, putting the children in control of the computer and, consequently, their own learning. It is therefore useful to once again summarise the contribution that LOGO can make to teaching and learning. The main areas that can be developed and supported are:

- Problem solving
- Development of investigation skills
- Logical thinking – thinking in an ordered way
- Cause-and-effect thinking
- Spatial awareness
- Collaborative learning
- Social skills, e.g. taking turns at working the computer or turtle
- Speaking and listening
- Editing skills
- Reading extension skills
- Estimation skills
- Mental arithmetic skills, e.g. number bonds
- Direction
- Angles and bearings
- Shape and space.

The theory of LOGO and the connection to Jean Piaget

In order to fully appreciate how LOGO can support the above-mentioned aspects of education, it is necessary to briefly explain the underlying theory of LOGO. This will enable users to understand how Seymour Papert's original philosophy connects with everyday classroom practice.

Although perhaps out of fashion at the moment, nevertheless most teachers will be aware of the work of the Swiss psychologist Jean Piaget, and his influential writings on the ways that children develop cognitively. His researches into children's learning, and his analysis that children develop through a series of distinct stages, and that their intellectual development is dependent upon reaching these stages, are well known. After studying with Piaget, Papert became impressed with his way of 'looking at children as active builders of their own intellectual structures' (Papert, 1980, p.19), and as a result he developed the LOGO programming language for use with children at the Massachusetts Institute of Technology (MIT). The underlying idea of the use of a floor or screen turtle was based around the idea that it would provide a link so that children would be able to move more easily from the 'concrete operational' stage of Piaget's hypothesis, where 'hands-on' first-hand experience is required for learning to occur, through to the more formal, or abstract, stages. However, unlike Piaget, Papert felt that given the right conditions and environments, children's progress through these stages of intellectual development could be accelerated. As a result of this belief, he developed LOGO specifically for this purpose. The use of the floor turtle directly connects to the concrete operational stage, and the use of the repeat and procedure functions in a screen LOGO directly connects to the more formal or abstract stages of development. We have already mentioned the importance of pupils having a say in their own learning and, in particular, learning by discovery. LOGO ideally reinforces this approach. As Papert himself stated, '... in a LOGO environment, new ideas are often acquired as a means of satisfying a personal need to do something one could not do before' (Papert, 1980, p. 74).

This is immediately reinforced by the cause-and-effect notion, where children can see immediately the result of their collaborative discussion and their subsequent inputs.

It therefore becomes important for the teacher to understand the theories upon which the philosophy is based, as the teacher needs to appreciate the relative connections between the children's stages of development and the associated ICT tasks. This ensures that learning activities and the associated tasks are pitched at an appropriate level, and that effective learning will result. It is also important to remember that the teacher needs to focus clearly upon the learning that results from the use of a turtle, not the technology itself. Even though this is basically a graphics package, we have already seen that the finished drawings are not great art and, in this outcome-orientated age, this might not always be appreciated by those who are constantly looking out for evidence of the phrases of the moment: 'quality assurance' or 'standards'. However, we have already seen that the power of LOGO cannot be underestimated.

The relationship between teacher and learner has to include the development of logical thinking. This means the ability to reason and to make sensible judgements in a range of situations, the development of investigative skills, and the ability to be able to approach and tackle a task in order to solve a problem. In order to do this effectively both teacher and the child as the learner need to have good communication skills and to be able to work collaboratively. The teacher needs to be able to indicate how the learner needs to develop. Teachers will need to help their pupils edit and refine their LOGO responses. For their part the learners need to be able to interact with their peers. As we have already mentioned in previous chapters, the use of LOGO can actively develop these social skills, not only for use within the LOGO environment, but across other subjects too; again, though, this has to occur within defined roles. This chapter will discuss why this is so.

It is the belief of the authors that the fundamental skills that should underpin all good primary teaching are the development of key problem-solving skills, such as the ability to hypothesise, predict, investigate, observe and record. These are skills that are not the sole preserve of LOGO, or even of mathematics. Unfortunately, these seem to have been, to a greater or lesser degree, lost during the course of the introduction firstly of the National Curriculum and then the National Numeracy Strategy. (It is an interesting informal observation on the part of the authors that LOGO was widely used in British primary schools during the 1980s, when computers were very limited in comparison to the specifications of modern computer equipment, yet the moment that LOGO was specifically mentioned in the very first mathematics document in 1989 it virtually disappeared overnight.) It seems strange that a tool that can genuinely develop such a wide range of basic mathematical skills in a completely integrated and meaningful way is not more widely used. There is a need for children to be able to hypothesise, predict, investigate, observe and record, all of which are so often engendered by collaborative learning and the engagement in dialogues of a 'what if ...' nature. It is this collaborative process and the associated discussion that demand a greater intellectual involvement from the child. Consequently, there is a need for the teacher to be able to facilitate these processes.

The role of the teacher

If LOGO is to be utilised to its fullest extent then the place and role of the teacher becomes crucial. The main challenge for the teacher is to provide the children with a 'real life' setting within which to solve a problem. In order for the learners to fully explore and exploit the potential that LOGO can offer as a learning experience, it is important that the teacher acts as a facilitator to new learning and, most importantly, as a means of accessing higher levels of this new learning. In some cases, this may well mean some modification of teaching style and philosophy on the part of the teacher. Given the hands-on emphasis within LOGO, it might be expected that the teacher has a relatively small role to play. Because of the collaborative nature of the process, it might also be expected that the children as learners will be able to devise and complete their own investigations, be able to debug as appropriate and thus carry the process through to a logical and meaningful conclusion. However, as any experienced primary school teacher knows, this is not likely to be the case. Learning situations such as this demand a high level of planning, preparation and interaction on the part of the teacher. This in turn means that the teacher has to become particularly skilled in several aspects of the use of LOGO. These include two key areas. The most important of these is that the teacher has to have a detailed knowledge and understanding of LOGO's place and purpose within the curriculum in general, and what she or he is trying to achieve in that lesson or sequence of lessons in particular. The teacher will need to have a good understanding of the place and purpose of LOGO in a holistic sense; i.e. the need to be aware how LOGO can develop the children's whole learning process. This includes generic skills such as, for example, teaching the children to structure investigations in order to solve and identify problems, and to suggest solutions and carry out fair tests. These skills can be applied right across the primary school curriculum – science and technology being the two most obvious examples. The second important factor is that the teacher has to be able to appreciate the contribution that LOGO can make to that lesson or sequence of lessons in terms of the specific subject objectives. These might include numeracy, shape and space, and angles and bearings in mathematics, or it may enhance the learning of language through discussion, speaking and listening, as well as producing commands concisely and in sequence.

The importance of questioning

We have already seen that one of the principal key aspects of the teacher's role within LOGO is the need to not only ask the right question, but to ask it in the right way. This therefore reinforces the need for the teacher to have a very good knowledge of LOGO in the ways discussed above. As with any subject, if teachers have a detailed knowledge of any topic that is being taught, they are in a stronger position to teach it effectively. They are more confident in their preparation and delivery, and they will be flexible in that they can adjust the pace and direction of the lesson easily. Factors influencing this might include the needs of the pupils, the time allocated to the lesson, previous learning and available resources.

This flexibility is particularly important whenever any process-orientated curriculum is taught. LOGO is no exception. As an interactive topic, the nature of the question that the teacher poses is very important for successful learning to take place. We have already seen that open-ended questions of the 'What if …?' type are important in this kind of teaching and learning situation. This is because, in this instance, the role of the teacher is primarily to extend children's thinking. A closed question, perhaps asking how many steps will place the turtle under a chair, or how many degrees the turtle needs to be turned, is entirely appropriate in a particular context. However, this type of question should largely be confined to a supplementary role, and used as a secondary question in order to reinforce the key idea or objective being taught during that particular lesson or sequence of lessons. In the wider context open-ended questioning should always be employed. Some examples of questions for LOGO might include:

- 'What would happen if the turtle is turned another 10 degrees?'
- 'What would happen if the turtle is moved forward another 30 steps?'
- 'How could this square be turned into a rectangle?'

There are innumerable permutations of searching, open-ended questions. It is very important for the teacher to ensure that the activities are set in situations that lend themselves to this kind of focussed questioning and this type of teaching and learning. There is little point in setting up activities that require a high level of intellectual and mathematical thought to complete, yet are not matched by the level of teacher questioning or, indeed, input. Too many opportunities for powerful and relevant learning will be lost amongst closed, superficial questioning that does little to extend the thinking processes of the learners. This applies to children of all ages, and not just those at the top end of Key Stage 2, where it is often assumed that this type of learning can only take place. Indeed, it can apply to any age of child, and to any topic or subject. We discussed in an earlier chapter the need for the child to be interactive with the computer. It is also critical to ensure that the teacher remains interactive with the pupils. Indeed, rarely in ICT and mathematics is there a greater need for there to be a three-way interactive triangle involving the ICT resources being used, the teacher and the learner. Sample activities might include, with a Year 1 group of children:

- 'I want you to make the turtle travel around all four lilypads, starting and finishing at the same place.'

This in turn could lead to appropriate interventions such as:

- 'How many steps do you think the turtle will have to travel in total?'
- 'How many commands do you think you will need to use?'

And then, when the children have entered the commands one step at a time, they could be asked to try to enter all of the commands in one go. Appropriate questions then might be:

- 'How many turns will the turtle make?'
- 'What sorts of shapes can you make out of four corners and sides?'
- 'How long do you think that it will take to travel to all four places?'

Questions such as these extend the learning process and bring real quality to the teaching and learning situation.

A group of Year 3 children may be asked:

- 'Using First Logo, I want you to draw a picture or object on the screen. It can be anything that you like.'

Once the children begin this, preferably in pairs, the teacher can listen into the children's conversations. The teacher should hear earnest discussion on whether the turtle should be moved left or right, forwards or backwards, how many steps it should be moved to join two lines together or how many degrees it should be turned. Even after 20 years, the authors remain surprised at the high level of mathematical discussion that takes place in these situations, from pupils and adults of all ages. Appropriate comments might include:

- 'That's a good drawing. Tell me how you drew it. Why did you do it in that way?'
- 'That's nice. Tell me about it.'

The main purpose of this approach is to get the children thinking about what they have done and why they have done it. This deconstruction of their own learning enables them to think about how they are using the package and its functions and about the kinds of decisions that they are making. From this point, increasingly focussed and detailed questions can be asked about specific aspects of their work, which in turn can form the basis for assessing the children's achievement.

Assessing LOGO

The learning experiences that are offered to the children need to be matched to their developmental requirements and levels of understanding. In order to do this the teacher will need to use a range of previous assessments as well as references to their records of attainment. This may mean consulting the pupil's achievements in other areas of the curriculum or, in the specific case of LOGO, it will mean looking at formative assessments of previous LOGO activities.

Generally speaking, any assessments of LOGO will be formative assessments, and involve the teacher assessing the children as they work. The open-ended and process-orientated nature of LOGO means that assessments normally have to be undertaken as the work is progressing. As we have already seen, the finished LOGO graphics rarely tell the whole story. For a start, as we have already mentioned, they will not be great art. There may be little or no record of the way in which the images were produced, and such as there is may well be incorporated into the final draft if the debugging process has already taken place. Therefore it will not illustrate the many refinements and revisions that any particular piece of work may have required. In addition to all this, as the work will probably have been produced as a direct result of collaborative effort, the teacher will need to assess in a formative way to discover each of the children's respective contributions to the work. Summative assessment methods cannot often be easily used for this purpose.

Appreciating continuity and progression in LOGO

In any classroom project, particularly a practical one, the teacher needs to be both a facilitator and an instructor. The former ensures that the processes of learning as well as the day-to-day 'mechanics' of classroom management are carried out; the latter enables in the widest possible sense, the children to understand the subject matter, be it mathematics or food technology. In the role of facilitator, when observing a group of children using LOGO, in whatever context, be it a floor or screen turtle, or even when programming a control technology model using a control box and associated software, the teacher needs to be able to decide at what point it may become appropriate to intervene. This is a crucial skill. When watching children working on a task, it can become very tempting to jump in and give them the correct answer. This should be resisted at all costs. The whole point of LOGO is that the children debug their own work. Therefore, it is appropriate that the teacher guides the learners in the correct direction, but without actually giving away the solution to the problem that is being tackled. This is in no way a shirking of the teachers' role, or their responsibilities. It simply enables the children to have a say in their own learning and it allows them to reflect, analyse and evaluate this learning. To develop this, the teacher needs to encourage the children to re-enter the cycle of evaluation and re-evaluation at progressively higher levels to enable them to develop and extend their own learning.

The teacher needs to be able to understand the continuity and progression within LOGO through knowing which particular aspects of LOGO build upon one another in a coherent way. In the first instance, when using the floor turtle, the teacher should begin the LOGO experience by using single commands to produce a result. This might involve simply moving the floor turtle from one point to another, or using a screen turtle to draw, in progressive stages, a shape or series of irregular shapes, such as a house. These single commands are then linked together to form a sequence of commands, perhaps entered in one operation to produce a shape or shapes at the click of one button. The user then progresses to the use of repeat commands, so that one shape can be drawn, rotated and repeated any number of times to produce a new, and different, geometric shape altogether. Even allowing for the fact that the teacher will probably be teaching a group of children of about the same age, it is useful to appreciate and understand which particular aspects of LOGO will have been taught previously and will be taught later. Quite apart from a need to differentiate within any particular class of children, a wider view of the progression of LOGO is necessary, in order to place the work into the broad context of LOGO learning experiences.

Consequently, progression should be logical, build upon previous learning experiences and be free of gaps in terms of LOGO operating skills and conceptual understanding. This in turn means that the teacher recognises this continuity and progression and applies it to the teaching and learning situation. Medium-term plans have therefore to be written upon a clear understanding of what the teacher intends to achieve across a whole series of lessons.

The role of the learner

In the same way that teachers have a clear role when teaching LOGO, so children have a distinct role as learners. With the assistance of the teacher as facilitator, they have to learn how to 'think LOGO'. This means that they have to be able to act on their own initiative, work as part of a team in a collaborative manner, be prepared to edit their own work and to accept that mistakes, or debugging, are an integral part of the learning process. Children may need considerable encouragement to work in this way and, as a result, it can be difficult for the child to appreciate that a mistake is not necessarily a bad thing. If teachers have to modify the way they teach in order to deliver LOGO effectively, then children also need to develop the confidence to engage in higher-order skills such as editing and debugging their work to get the desired response from the turtle.

For the child in the Reception Class this may involve having the confidence to suggest how to make the turtle move around a play mat, or to work co-operatively with other members of the class. For the older child this could involve editing a series of complex procedures using a screen-based LOGO package, perhaps by entering and re-entering the development cycle several times in order to refine a series of commands to produce the desired response. In both cases children need to be able to work independently, and take autonomous decisions. Although the teacher remains an integral part of the learning process, the pupil–teacher relationship changes from the kinds of didactic teaching and learning that often occur as a result of rigidly following the national strategies.

A long-term **LOGO** case study

The authors' thanks go to Bob Hopcraft, the Headteacher and ICT Co-ordinator at St Nicholas (VA) Primary School, Letchworth Garden City, Hertfordshire, and to all the teachers involved, particularly the school's Maths Co-ordinator, Kate Page, for this case study.

The unit of work described here forms part of the school's Autumn Term ICT and Numeracy programme. It lasts six weeks, with children working in the ICT suite for two sessions each week. The suite is equipped with 15 pupil machines and one teacher machine linked to an interactive whiteboard. The machines are peer-to-peer networked, and children work in pairs to aid discussion and skill-sharing.

This unit of work is designed to extend the children's understanding of shape and space, and to develop their basic programming skills. These are built upon the work previously carried out in Year 2 with the floor turtle. Overall, the complete programme is allied closely to the Year 4 Qualifications and Curriculum Authority (QCA) ICT unit, 'Modelling effects on screen'; however the school took the decision to spread the work over a three-year period, to allow the children more time to develop a deeper understanding of LOGO programming. Thus the floor turtle work is done in Year 2, with the introduction to the screen turtle (using *MSW Logo*) in Year 3 as described here. This allows the children to explore the program in greater depth, so that in Year 4 they can be introduced to writing procedures and to recursion.

This case study describes work carried out by Year 3 children, and is by its very nature experimental. Thus the children have the opportunity to explore and 'play' with *MSW Logo*, and use it to support their knowledge and understanding of shape and space and directional language. Hence the work is linked closely to the relevant programme for numeracy (which, in Year 3 is Measures, Shape and Space). It also helps the more able children to prepare for those objectives that follow in Year 4.

Introduction to the screen turtle

The children are encouraged to try and draw a square, with the minimum of help from the teacher. They have already had practice in Year 2 at manoeuvring the floor turtle, but now they have to translate it to the screen. The introduction to this is usually done as a whole-class activity, using the interactive whiteboard, in order that the teacher can demonstrate the various movements that the turtle can make, and how these are programmed. The children then work at their individual computers and draw squares of various sizes, using one command at a time. The time for this process obviously varies according to the ability of the children; however, no more than two sessions are normally required. During this time the children, if they have mastered the 'one command at a time' procedure, are also encouraged to write further commands, so that they become aware of what effects these have on the screen turtle. If they wish, they can jot these commands down in their notebooks or, alternatively, work directly onto the screen. By this stage the more able children can write the whole procedure for a square, whilst others will program it in shorter stages (see Figures 6.1 and 6.2).

```
fd 100 rt 90 fd 100 rt 90 fd 100
rt 90 fd 100
pu fd 100
pd fd 100 rt 90 fd 100 rt 90 fd 100
rt 90 fd 100
ft
ht
```

Figure 6.1 Two squares drawn with *MSW Logo*, and the commands that were used to create them.

```
fd 100
rt 90
fd 150
fd 10
fd 100
rt 90 fd 100
rt 90
fd 150
fd 10
fd 100
rt 90
```

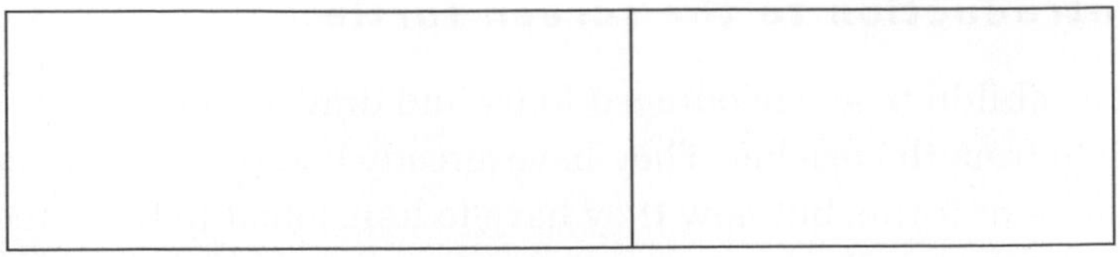

Figure 6.2 Two rectangles drawn with *MSW Logo*, and the commands that were used to create them.

Usually, by the beginning of the third session, the children can be encouraged to choose an upper-case letter that contains right angles, (such as E, F, H, I, and T), and are asked to draw their enlarged letter on the screen (see Figures 6.3 to 6.5). This can be a very demanding process. To move the turtle in the right direction, as well as making allowances for the variation in the lengths of the lines, requires the children to utilise all their new skills, as well as needing a good deal of spatial awareness and understanding. Because of this, the initial approach is again experimental; as Bob Hopcraft explains, 'Rather akin to "doodling" on the screen, and this session usually involves plenty of false starts'. However, as their skills develop, the children are able to attempt more than one command at a time, and are encouraged to keep a permanent record

```
fd 100
rt 90
fd 30
lt 90
fd 30
lt 90
fd 50
fd 20
lt 90
fd 30
lt 90
fd 10
fd 10
rt 90
fd 100
lt 10
lt 80
fd 10
fd5
I don't know how  to fd5
fd 5
fd 5
ht
st
ht
```

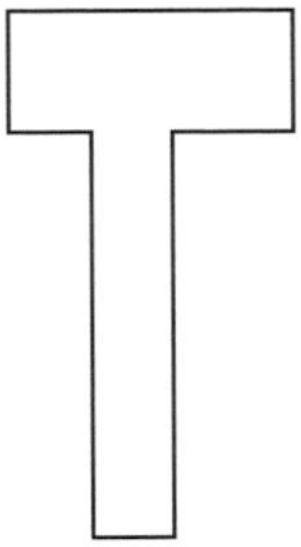

Figure 6.3 The letter 'T' drawn with *MSW Logo* and the commands that produced it.

```
fd 100
lt 90
f
I don't know how  to f
fd 100
rt 90
fd 20
rt 90
fd 100
fd 100
rt 90
fd 20
rt 90
fd 80
lt 90
fd 100
rt 90
fd 20
ht
```

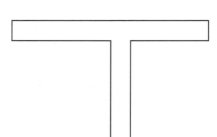

Figure 6.4 Another letter 'T' drawn with *MSW Logo*, and the commands that produced it.

```
fd 100
rt 90
fd 20
rt 90
fd 80
lt 90
fd 80
rt 90
rd 20
I don't know how  to rd
fd 20
rt 90
rd 100
I don't know how  to rd
fd 100
```

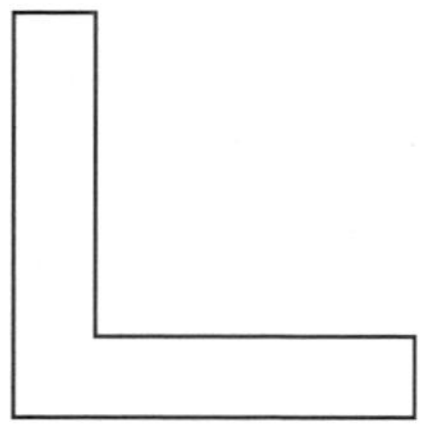

Figure 6.5 The letter 'L' drawn with *MSW Logo*, and the commands that produced it.

of these in their notebooks. At this stage, as well as encouraging the children to draw various other shapes containing right angles, the teacher might also demonstrate a RIGHT 45 command, for those children who wish to draw more ambitious shapes. However, we are well aware that this is a process which cannot be hurried, and that at this stage, in particular, time must be allowed for the children to consolidate their understanding of spatial awareness. This is an abstract idea that forms slowly, and only after the children have experienced many and various related activities, including play. It is not the same as learning basic computer skills. As an aid to this, the children are encouraged to download *MSW Logo* from the Internet at home, so that they can practise and extend their skills out of school time.

During the final sessions the children are introduced to the REPEAT command. They quickly see this as a useful tool, as it enables them to complete their regular shapes more quickly. As a special 'treat' they are finally introduced to the formula REPEAT x [FD y RT 360/x]. This allows them to draw regular polygons, making the necessary adjustments so that they fit the screen, as well as enabling them to utilise their understanding of the properties of shapes learned during their mathematics lessons. Two examples are illustrated by Figures 6.6 and 6.7.

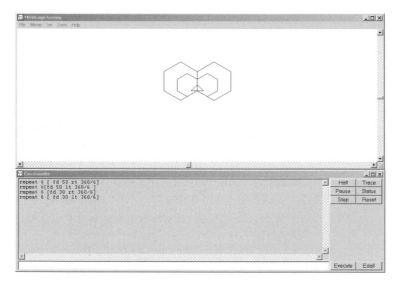

Figure 6.6 Two hexagons with commands.

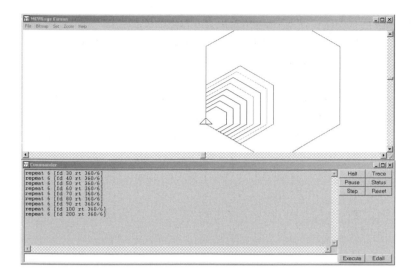

Figure 6.7 Repeating hexagonal patterns drawn with *MSW Logo*.

Conclusion

LOGO encapsulates all that is best in child-centred learning. However, once the children have mastered the skills required to work the floor turtle, and have later become conversant with the screen turtle programs, it can hardly be anything else but child-centred. LOGO has the added advantage in that children can use it for a wide range of other mathematics, whilst still being within the dictates of the National Curriculum in both mathematics and ICT, as well as the requirements of the National Numeracy Strategy.

Bibliography

DfEE/QCA, *Information and Communication Technology: The National Curriculum for England*, HMSO, London, 1999.

Papert, S., *Mindstorms: Children, Computers and Powerful Ideas*, second edition, Harvester Wheatsheaf, London, 1980.

Chapter 7

Handling data

In our previous book, *ICT and Primary Science* (Williams and Easingwood, 2003), we described in detail the three types of database that we felt were suitable for use in primary schools:

1   The Free Text Database, used to search for information on the World Wide Web or a CD-ROM. Here the children use the 'search' function of the Web page or software to find specific information.
2   Branching or Binary Tree Database, a hierarchical branching database which allows information to be retrieved through the use of questions that require a simple yes or no answer.
3   Random Access Database, which not only stores the data, but enables refined systematic searching and interrogation. This is the type of database that will be familiar to many teachers.

We also described in detail the structure and usage of spreadsheets: how they can not only list and display data, but how they can mathematically utilise this information to produce further information such as totals, averages and measurements. As with a database, this information can be displayed in various forms.

The handling of data can involve any of these programs, However, the children must first have some data to handle. We strongly advocate that the original data should be collected by the children themselves, during a hands-on, practical activity. The handling of data is not simply making lists. It involves analysing the information, and often extrapolating the results to reach definite and defined conclusions. This can only be done with real and relevant data, however simple it might be. If the data are just made up for the lesson, then the subsequent work will have far less meaning and relevance for the children.

Data handling and the curriculum

It is worth taking a close look at both the Numeracy Hour and the National Curriculum requirements for mathematics, and take note of just how much they seem to contradict each other. Which is considered to be the most important? Schools do not have to teach the Numeracy Hour (or the Literacy Hour for that matter), but they do by law have to follow the requirements of the National Curriculum. However, it takes some confidence to discard either or both of these 'hours', particularly when the SATS come round. We are certainly not advocating that any written 'official' curriculum should be ignored. However, we do think that when planning lessons, either in the long or short term, teachers should be fully conversant with what is in print, and where possible adapt it to the particular needs of their children. There is much to interest any teacher in the Numeracy Hour (let alone the children), but teachers need to ask questions of it, such as: does it omit areas of mathematics that would be of value to primary children, and which might benefit everyone by introducing them at an early stage?

The authors feel strongly that there are such areas, but realise that with the curriculum overloaded as it is, teachers would hardly be sympathetic to the idea of increasing their workload, or indeed that of the children. However, we feel it is possible to widen the scope of primary mathematics through the proper use of ICT, and in further chapters we will suggest ways in which this can be done. For the moment let us consider the curriculum in relation to data handling alone.

If we look at the National Curriculum we find that there is one whole section in Key Stage 2 which is set aside for the handling, applying, representing and interpreting of data. In Key Stage 1, there are sub-sections which also require these processes. If we turn to the Numeracy Hour, we find that from Year 3 onwards there is a small section given over to the handling of data, and even earlier, from Year 1, there are sections for the organising and using of data. However, when this is compared with all the other work to be covered, it is difficult to see how the data used can be anything other than collections of prepared facts. Our contention is that data required for this kind of work, if it is to be fully understood, needs to be gathered by the children from real situations. Such real-life situations are not contrary to the ideas of the Numeracy Hour. In Year 1, for example, teachers are required to provide real-life problems involving money and measuring.

How then can teachers involve pupils in collecting their own data? There are several possibilities:

- To include extra mathematics in the timetable.
- To teach the Numeracy Hour for only three or at most four days of the week, and to use the other days for this kind of mathematics.
- To use other subjects, such as science, to obtain and analyse data.
- To use the ICT lesson, if one is included in the timetable, to gather and analyse the required data.

Of these options, we would not advocate the use of the first one. The idea of asking children to spend so much of their time on one subject, even when it is made as interesting as possible, is counter-productive. We have seen this attempted with the Literacy Hour followed by another 40 minutes of story writing. The results did not warrant the effort. We shall presume that any further work described will be based on one of the other three options.

A science-based topic – the third option

It is possible to describe the handling and interpreting of data as a series of mathematical processes which can be enhanced by the use of ICT. Obviously the original data may not in fact be 'mathematical', i.e. numerical. It could be a series of pictures, maps, or even a collection of artefacts. However, for these to be properly investigated, it may be necessary to somehow represent them as numbers, so that the subsequent data can be interpreted and fully understood.

For instance, a Year 6 class may, as part of an animal study, need to measure the relationship between the surface area of an animal and its volume. This relationship is a very important factor in all life sciences. It can govern the very existence of an organism from the smallest to the largest. Very often an organism can only exist in its particular environmental niche because of its size, be it large, small or even microscopic. However, in order to do its job, or even survive, it may have to pay a biological penalty appropriate to its size. Our red blood cells need to have a very large surface area to 'collect' the oxygen, yet they are of course very small. On a larger scale, a shrew needs to eat about four times its weight in food, every day. It is a small, active animal, and because it has a large surface area in relation to its volume, it loses heat (energy) rapidly, and without a high food intake would soon die. At the opposite end of the size scale, the elephant has a different problem – how to get rid of heat or, to put it more simply, how to keep cool. Despite appearances, because of its size an elephant has a small surface area in relation to its volume. So to increase this surface area, it has large ears, equipped with many blood vessels. When outspread, the blood can be cooled.

An interesting aspect of the surface area to volume ratio can even involve the humble (potato) chip. A large chip, because of its larger volume and relatively small surface area, will absorb less fat than the so-called thinner 'French fry'.

Although this may originate as a science topic, for those teachers who still try to cross subject boundaries and follow the currently out-of-fashion integrated-topic approach, this topic soon becomes one of practical mathematics. The authors have found that children can be highly motivated by this kind of project. It may be a science-based approach, but from the very start involves mathematical concepts and processes. If children have had any contact with animals at all, this example should be well within their experience. The shrew is about the size of a matchbox, so we can start with this as a mathematical approximation. (The, slightly larger, class gerbil will do if there is one.) All the children need to do is to draw a net of the correct size, and measure the surface area of the net (one part at a time, and then add them together). When this is complete, they fold the net into its cuboid shape, and measure its volume (see Figure 7.1).

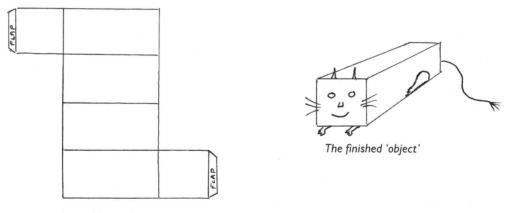

A suitable net for a mouse

The finished 'object'

Figure 7.1 A drawing of a net and complete cuboid animal.

The authors are well aware that some children, even in Year 6, can find measuring areas, let alone volumes, quite difficult. However, this is a project best done as a group activity, where at least one pupil in each group can manage the mathematics. Better still, whilst still keeping it a group-based activity, the actual calculations can be worked out by the complete class, guided by the teacher. Whatever method is used, we have found that this approach provides great motivation for children to understand the mathematics, perhaps because they see it in a completely different context from the usual mathematics lesson. It may even be that, for some, the enjoyment of making cuboid animals is worth a little mental effort.

To collect further data, other 'animals' need to be made. It is not difficult to estimate the size of a cat, or a school rabbit (many schools still keep them) or even a small dog. The size need only be an estimation, as surely all children have some knowledge of these animals. We may need two more in order to cover the normal range of sizes, and we suggest that they should be a human and an elephant. To build an approximation of an average sized human is quite easy, an elephant more difficult! However, contacting a zoo should provide sufficient information. This would also provide a useful opportunity to involve other aspects of ICT, such as e-mails and the Internet.

Let us summarise the topic so far. We now have examples of cuboid animals, and have a collection of interesting data. We have the surface area of each animal compared with its volume. The children will have made their models, and in order to do so will have drawn the net of the cube according to the approximate size of the animals that they have chosen. For the larger examples they will have either used a pile of equal-sized boxes to represent the human, or may have measured one of their friends, or even their teacher. The authors have even seen children wrap one of their class in newspaper so as to make an accurate measurement for the surface area. The elephant's measurements may well have had to be done by estimation! During the calculations the children will need to use relatively large numbers. For this reason, they should be encouraged to use calculators where appropriate, and the numbers they use (which are based on approximations anyway), should be rounded up to the nearest ten, or even hundred. We have never found that children have difficulties with large numbers themselves, indeed they are often fascinated by them. They may find them difficult to calculate using pen and paper, but so do many adults – but then, no one says adults shouldn't use calculators.

So far the children will have:
- Carried out a scientific study of a group of animals, and in particular the scientific importance of surface area to volume relationships;
- Engaged in the mathematical and design skills of measuring, drawing and cutting;
- Engaged in the mathematical skills of measuring and multiplication in relation to the concepts of area and volume;
- Engaged with the idea of approximation.

Animal	Surface area cm²	Volume cm³
Shrew or gerbil	72	30
Cat	1400	3000
Human	45,000	500,000
Elephant	640,000	28,000,000

Figure 7.2 Table showing the figures taken from a topic carried out by children, taught by one of the authors.

The results of their work may look like Figure 7.2. Before the introduction of computers into primary schools, this would have been the end of the topic. They would have written up these results, and may well have drawn simple block graphs to help them reach some conclusions, for there are certainly some very interesting questions arising from this topic that need answers. The kind of questions that a project of this sort might engender are as follows:

1   'What is different about the two sets of measurements for the shrew from all the others?'
2   'What is the significance of the very large difference between the measurements of the elephant?'
3   'What size of animal would give us an equal surface-area-to-volume relationship?'
4   'Can we calculate a ratio between the surface area and volume for each of these animals?'
5   'If we found the average of these two sets of figures, would this give us the "perfect animal"?'

In the past children would have found considerable difficulty in sorting out the vertical axis of any graph with the range of figures from 30 to 28 million. It is only through the use of ICT that any sensible graphical results can easily be obtained, although we need to realise which of the graphs are the most appropriate, and which ones will help us to answer these questions. Some examples of these are illustrated in Figures 7.3 to 7.9.

Using ICT to find answers to the questions raised in the topic

If these questions are put to the children, many of them will come up with some interesting and thoughtful answers. However, teachers now have available computer programs which can deal with this data so they can highlight relevant points, and display the data in a variety of forms. This enables the children to utilise these results in order to come to a variety of conclusions. Whilst the first two questions can be answered by the straightforward observation of the

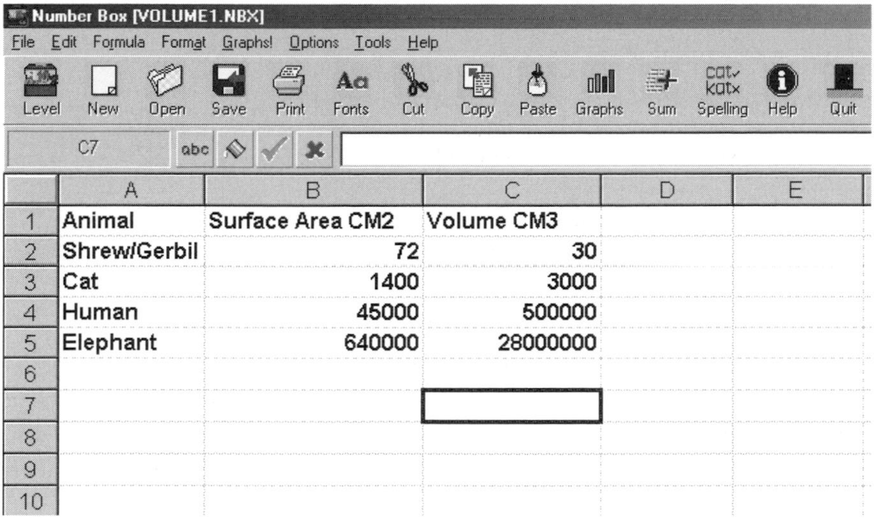

Figure 7.3 A screenshot of a spreadsheet from the *Black Cat* package *Number Box*. Step One: The data are entered onto a spreadsheet.

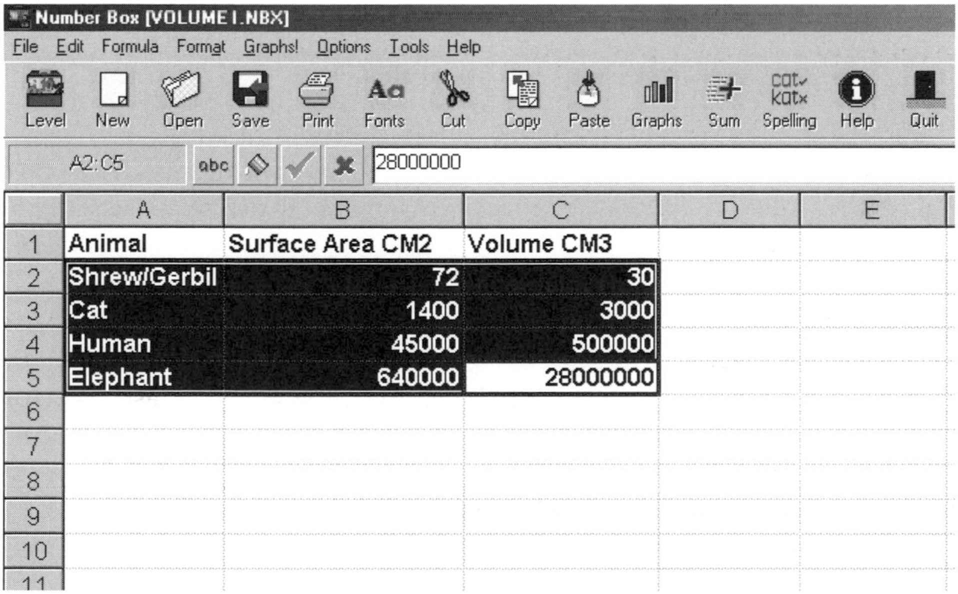

Figure 7.4 Step Two: the children highlight the area that you wish to graph. They avoid highlighting the titles as this upsets the 'shape' of the resulting graph.

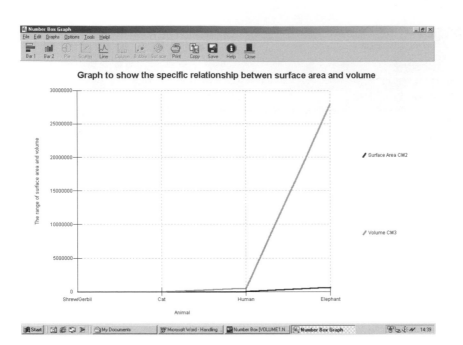

Figure 7.5 Step Three: a screenshot of *Number Box Graph* to illustrate the relationship between volume and surface area of the selected animals. The resulting graph is difficult to read and thus impossible to interpret accurately because the range between the smallest (shrew) and largest (elephant) is simply too large.

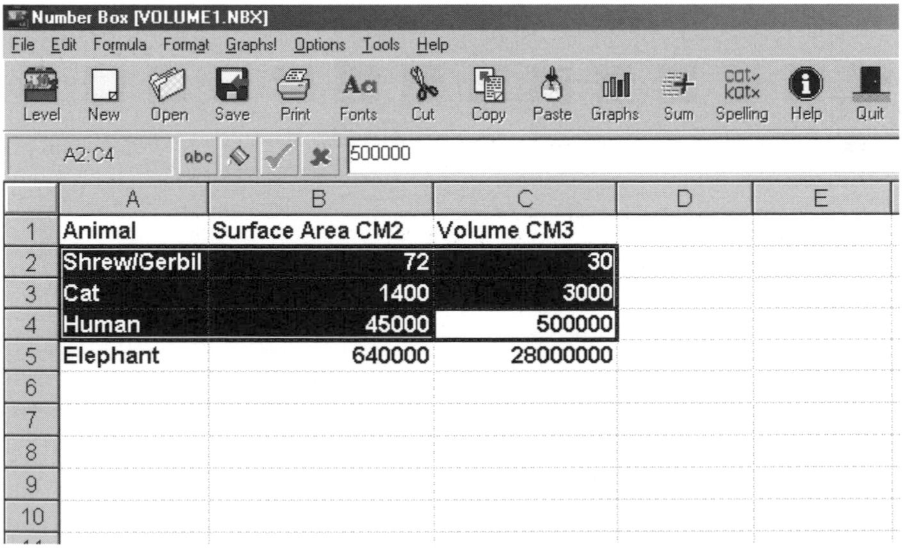

	A	B	C	D	E
1	Animal	Surface Area CM2	Volume CM3		
2	Shrew/Gerbil	72	30		
3	Cat	1400	3000		
4	Human	45000	500000		
5	Elephant	640000	28000000		
6					
7					
8					
9					
10					

Figure 7.6 Step Four: in order to narrow the range we have highlighted only three of the animals.

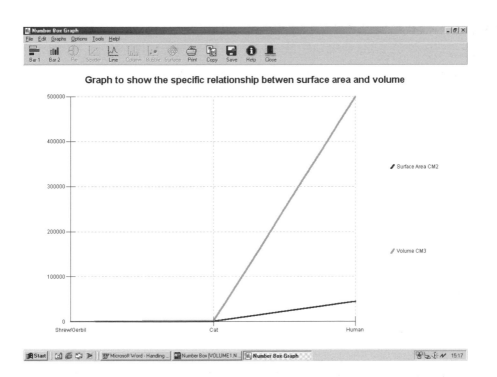

Figure 7.7 Step Five: although this gives a slightly clearer picture, we still need to know, with some precision, the exact point where the lines illustrating the volume and surface area coincide.

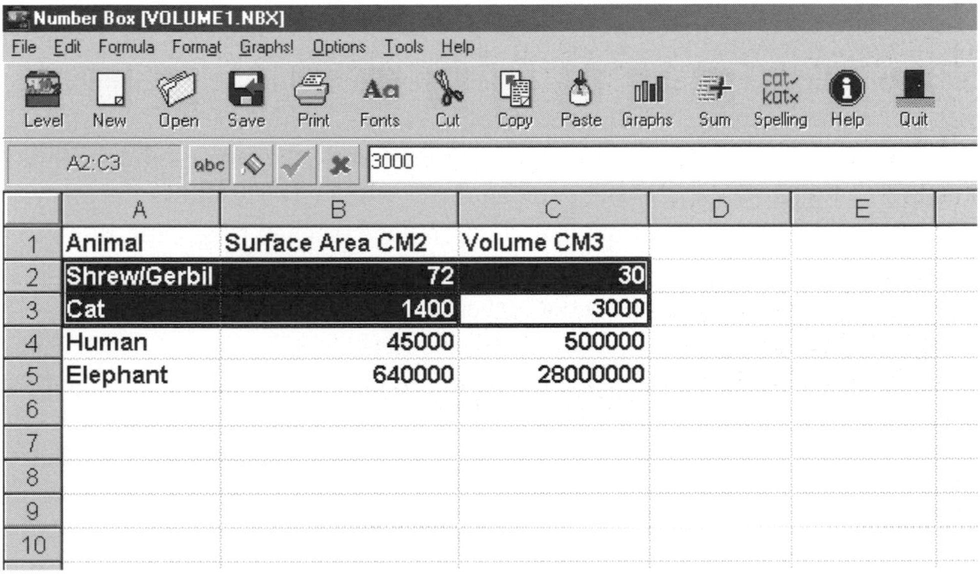

	A	B	C	D	E
1	Animal	Surface Area CM2	Volume CM3		
2	Shrew/Gerbil	72	30		
3	Cat	1400	3000		
4	Human	45000	500000		
5	Elephant	640000	28000000		
6					
7					
8					
9					
10					

Figure 7.8 Step Six: this time only two animals are highlighted.

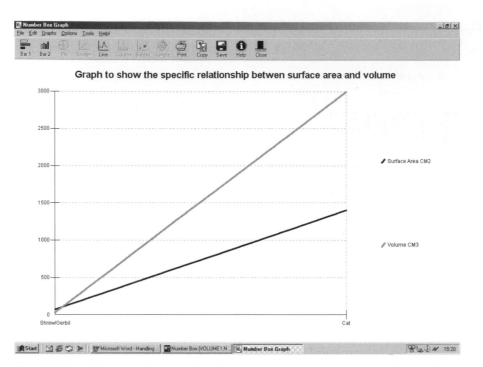

Figure 7.9 Step Seven: with the graph only showing two animals we can clearly see the specific relationship between the volume and the surface area and decide where, in the size scale, volume 'overtakes' surface area.

mathematical results obtained, the third example requires the processes and stages previously illustrated. Originally all the data were entered on to the spreadsheet, which was used as the basis for producing a series of graphs. The first graph produced (Figure 7.5) illustrated several limitations. It could not cope with the numerical range which extended from 30 to 28 million. However, by gradually reducing this range through the elimination of the larger animals, thus reducing the scale, we finally came to Figure 7.9 which clearly shows the answer to the third question. By the time that children have reached this point, they have built up a strong idea of the scientific concepts involved, enhanced their ICT skills, and have also developed a higher level of analytical insight.

One way of answering question 4 could be to produce four separate block graphs by highlighting the relevant data within the spreadsheet. These block graphs should be thought of as a way of illustrating the different proportions of surface area to volume. On a computer screen the colour will emphasise the particular proportions of the shrew's larger surface area to volume, relative to those of the other animals. This will involve highlighting the data for each animal in turn. It is therefore important to realise that what we are looking at in this series of block graphs is the proportionate size of each block (Figures 7.10 to 7.13).

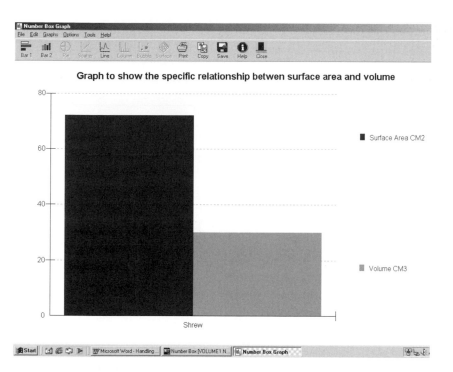

Figure 7.10 The shrew.

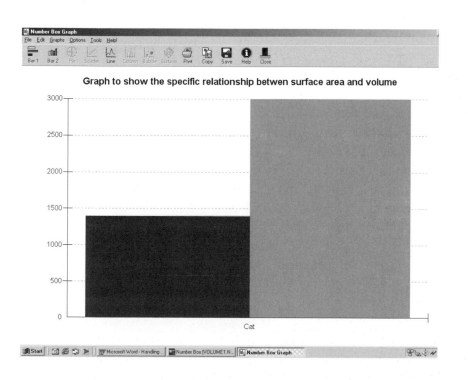

Figure 7.11 The cat.

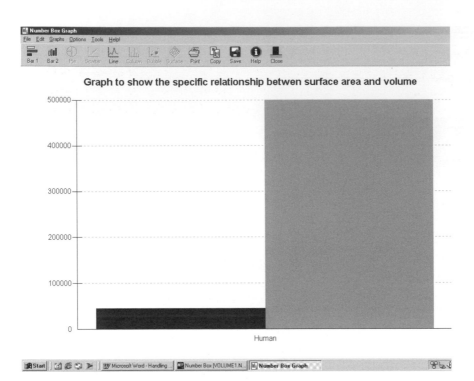

Figure 7.12 The human.

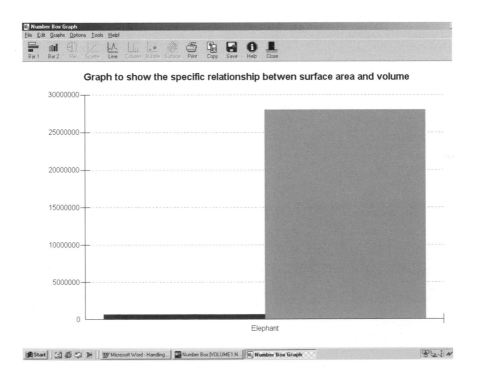

Figure 7.13 The elephant.

To answer question 5, we can use the capability of the spreadsheet to obtain the average and subsequently illustrate it in graphical form. Children can find the average by highlighting each column in turn, and then by using the 'Average' function of the spreadsheet. They can then calculate the average surface area and the average volume. This can then be displayed graphically, as illustrated in Figure 7.14.

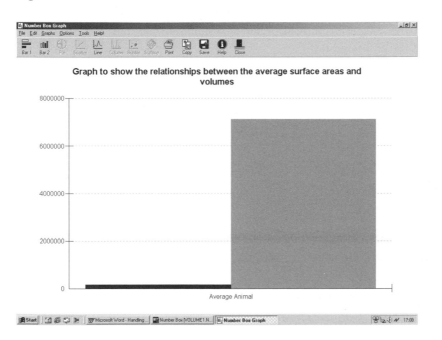

Figure 7.14 The relationships between the average surface areas and volumes.

Whether the idea of such an average is biologically correct is open to discussion, and could be a very valuable teaching point. What the authors hope is beyond doubt is that by reaching this stage the children would have attained a high level in the skills and understanding of both ICT and of mathematics.

It would be interesting to discuss with the children at this stage whether block graphs, as shown here, are appropriate for this information. It might be that a pie chart would show this more clearly if the program allows this option. We began this topic using block graphs. We continued using graphs as it seems to us that it is easier to compare two large blocks side by side on one graph than it would be to compare different segments of a pie chart. The appropriate use of pie charts is discussed in the next chapter.

Even if, for reasons of time, or level of skill or age of the children, it is not possible to produce work of this kind, it is still possible to carry out projects which fill the criteria suggested at the start of this chapter. Two of the case studies included below are just such examples. Each involved the collection of 'real' data, and both included considerable discussion, and some written work. Both were carried out by Key Stage 1 children, and while the ICT skills were commensurate with that age, the children showed a high level of understanding not only of how the computer should be used, but also how it can help to utilise and understand the collected data.

The case studies also illustrate how the whole process of data handling can be a part of the numeracy hour as well as utilising the limited time within the school timetable that is allowed for ICT by itself. Indeed, when necessary, both times were used to allow an integrated project.

Three case studies involving data handling software packages

Detailed below are three case studies collected from primary schools illustrating the use of a branching database, a random access database and a spreadsheet.

Using a branching database

Our thanks again to the children at St Nicholas C of E (VA) Primary School, Letchworth Garden City, Hertfordshire, and to Bob Hopcraft, the Headteacher and ICT Co-ordinator. We would also like to thank again the Mathematics Co-ordinator, Kate Page, and the Year 4 teacher Allys Bishop.

This project lasts six weeks, and is part of the Spring Term ICT and Numeracy Programme. It is also linked closely to the science taught in the school, particularly the unit containing the use of keys for identification.

The children would have been introduced to the use of a relational database in Year 3, but it is in Year 4 that they first confront the concepts of a branching system. The origins of this approach at the school actually predate the Qualifications and Curriculum Authority (QCA) ICT units, as well as the Numeracy Strategy, by some time, as the children in the fourth year have for several years studied a unit in mathematics entitled 'Decision Trees'. This taught the children to differentiate between up to 10 similar objects, by asking questions to which the answer could only be a 'yes' or a 'no'.

This is still the school's starting point, and the children quickly become adept at structuring their questions so that they are not in any way ambiguous. At this stage, the children are encouraged to work in groups, to construct and illustrate their decision trees on A1 sheets of paper, which are then displayed in the classroom. The children's plans can be very complex, often extending beyond the original 10 objects.

The children next move to the ICT suite to work in pairs, using the *Decisions 3* program. This was originally a program designed by *Black Cat* Software, but is now part of the *RM Window Box* package. Each pair is asked to choose a set of objects or animals (depending on the children's interests) as a basis for the construction of their branching database on the computer. Figures 7.15 to 7.19 show examples of branching databases.* At this stage the context of the project

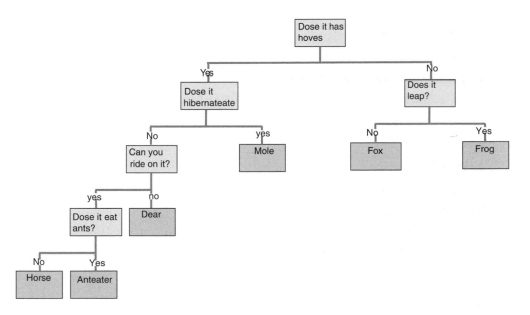

Figure 7.15 A branching database.

---

* The authors described the structure and use of a branching database in their book *ICT and Primary Science*. The potential for further work based on the binary 'yes' or 'no' requirements, described above, is also covered elsewhere in this book in Chapter 6.

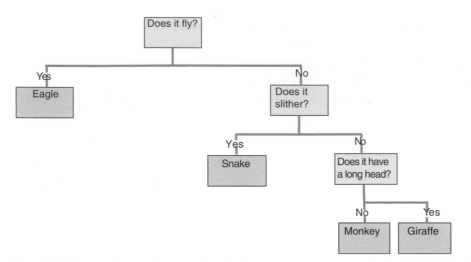

Figure 7.16 A branching database detailing 'yes' or 'no' answers to questions that identify different animals.

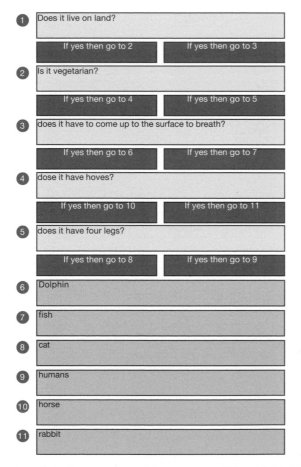

Figure 7.17 A screenshot of the summary of the 'Animals' branching database.

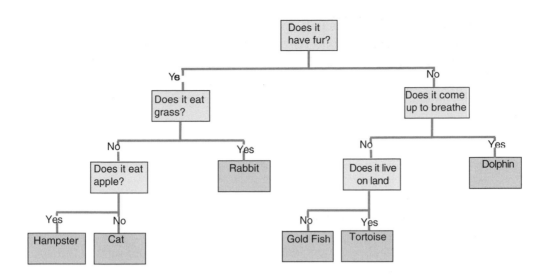

Figure 7.18 Another example of a branching database.

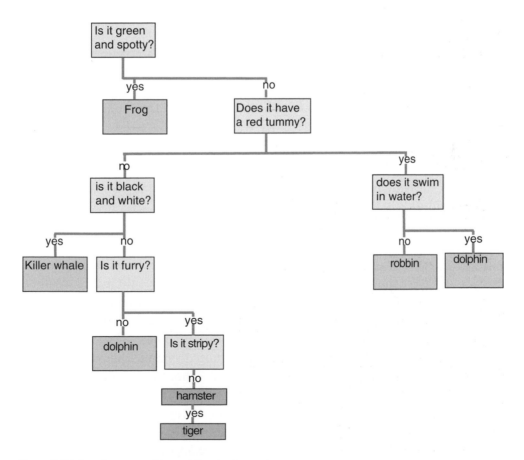

Figure 7.19 Another type of branching database structure.

can be restructured so as to include objects that have a direct mathematical content, such as shapes, different types of triangles, numbers and measures.

Finally, the children are encouraged to import clipart or pictures from the Internet to enhance their database, and then each pair shares their finished database with the rest of the class.

Using a database with Key Stage 1

Our thanks to Ash Tree Class, and their teacher, Sarah Cass, at Westbury Infant, Nursery and Primary School, Letchworth Garden City, Hertfordshire.

This Year 2 class of 28 children decided to investigate different kinds of footwear, and use a database for both recording and analysing their findings. The project required them to investigate a given sample of footwear – in this case their own – to see what might be the most popular type.

During a class discussion, the children decided to list the types of footwear under the following headings:

- Colour
- Size
- Type or style
- Design of fastening (or, in the children's words, 'How they were done up').

The project started with the whole class working with a blank pro-forma survey sheet, on which to collect the data.

Their teacher, with the help of the old-fashioned blackboard, illustrated in Figure 7.20, explained the exercise to the children. It was decided that each child should have their own database, and therefore each would record a sample of as many shoes as time allowed. An alternative would have been to record all 28 types of footwear on just one database. However, this would have meant that only a limited number of children would have been involved. By each child building his or her own database, even with a limited sample, they were all involved, and each had the opportunity to use the school's computers.

Once the children had collected their data on the survey sheet (Figures 7.21 and 7.22), they entered them onto the database (Figure 7.23). For this project the class used the Granada *Black Cat Information Workshop* database at the Red Level. It was at this stage that some of the most interesting work took place. The

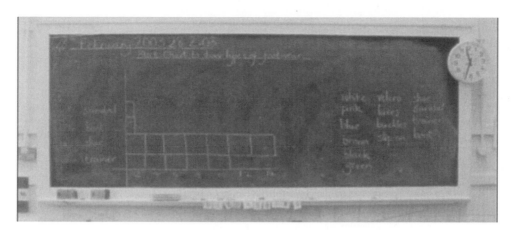

Figure 7.20 The old-fashioned blackboard.

Survey to find out about footwear.

Name	Type	Colour	Size	Fastening
Alex.	trainer	blue	1	laces
Brooklyn.	shoe	black	13	slip on
Miss Cass.	shoe	blue	6	slip on
Sarah.	trainer	white	12	laces
Jessica.	shoe	black	4	velcro
Amy	trainer	white	11	laces
Runah.	trainer	silver	13	velcro
maggie	shoe	black	3	slip on
Shannon	shoe	black	12	velcro
Kade	boot	black	10	laces
matthew	trainer	black	12	velcro

Figure 7.21 An example of one of the children's data collection sheets.

Figure 7.22 The children completing their data collection sheets

Figure 7.23 Two children entering their data onto a laptop computer.

class had to decide just how best this information should be displayed, e.g. a graph or a pie chart, and what would be the most suitable from a mathematical point of view.

At the time of writing, the class is producing a variety of different graphs and charts. They are having to decide what are the merits (or otherwise) of each, and which are the most mathematically correct. They also have to incorporate into their graphs sufficient information to make them viable, and decide on scales, axes and even using the correct headings. One interesting problem that they have to solve is how best to differentiate between children's and adult size shoes (it is not only adults that have adult-sized footwear). Figures 7.24 to 7.28 show this work in progress.

Figure 7.24 The teacher discusses with the children how best to interpret their data.

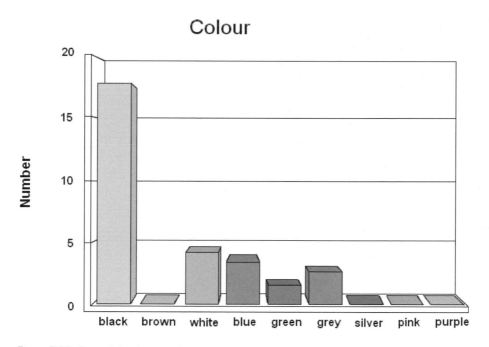

Figure 7.25 One of the first graphs to be produced was of simple colour differentiation.

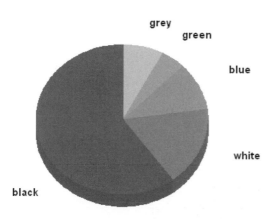

Figure 7.26 The children produced pie charts to see if they would show the information more clearly than a graph.

Fastening

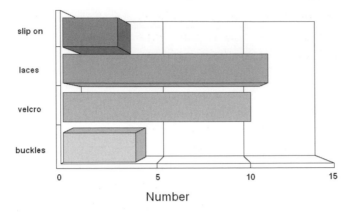

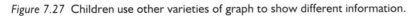

Fastening

Figure 7.27 Children use other varieties of graph to show different information.

Type

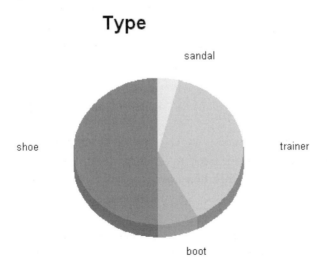

Figure 7.28 It can be seen from these examples that what began as a simple marketing project has now become a decidedly mathematical exercise.

A Year 5 spreadsheet case study

Thanks again to Bob Hopcraft, Headteacher of St Nicholas C of E (VA) School, Letchworth Garden City, Hertfordshire, and to the children and their teachers, Margaret Gilbert, the Deputy Head, and Kate Page, the Mathematics Co-ordinator.

Whenever possible, the school likes to encourage children to apply their numeracy skills to practical problems – wherever possible to those arising from real-life situations. The children become heavily involved in the planning for the annual Christmas Market, which is a joint fundraising event with the local church. They become involved in costing the baking of cakes, and calculating profit margins. The school also holds frequent 'non-uniform days' to raise money for various charities, and the income is counted and checked by various classes in the school. The children therefore have become used to this way of working by the time they reach Year 5, and even have an understanding of profit and loss.

The unit on spreadsheets forms a part of the school's Autumn Term ICT and Numeracy Programme, and relates closely to the QCA Unit 5D.

The children are introduced to *RM Number Magic* that is part of the *RM Window Box* package of programs, and their teacher demonstrates the cell system to them. Parallels are drawn with tables, graphs and co-ordinates with which all the children are familiar through previous experience. Initially, the children are encouraged to practise at producing lists and to classify information in a variety of ways. For example, the children use sheets to record their skill level at physical education and to record spelling and other scores. Their attention is drawn to the 'list view' in the relational database used in Year 3, which is in itself a spreadsheet.

It is at this stage that they are introduced to the idea of a formula, and the way in which this gives the spreadsheet its real power and meaning. They are encouraged to develop a range of different formulae. Here the emphasis is on 'play', albeit a little structured, for all children need to develop the confidence to experiment and try out for themselves any work experience involving concepts that are new to them.

As Christmas approaches, the project culminates in the children producing a Christmas list. They are given a ceiling figure and have to find out how many Christmas gifts, decorations, cards, and other relevant items, they can buy with

Item	cost	number	total cost
turkey	£3.00	2	£6.00
xmas tree	£10.00	1	£10.00
lights	£0.20	2	£0.40
wreath	£0.11	3	£0.33
baubles	£0.50	5	£2.50
cards	£1.00	3	£3.00
presents	£6.00	1	£6.00
chocolate	£4.00	2	£8.00
tree top	£1.00	1	£1.00
angel	£0.50	5	£2.50
c-pudding	£0.90	9	£8.10
stocking	£2.00	2	£4.00
sweets	£0.50	1	£0.50
ice cream	£3.00	2	£6.00
cakes	£0.90	4	£3.60
tinsel	£2.00	2	£4.00
bells	£2.00	3	£6.00
		total:	£71.93

Figure 7.29 An example of a spreadsheet detailing spending at Christmas. The first column details the item, the second the cost per unit, the third column details how many of each is purchased and the final column details the cost per item. The spreadsheet has been configured to multiply the costs in the second and third column and display it in the fourth column. The total cost is displayed in the bottom right cell. This has been set up by adding together all of the values in the fourth column.

their money (see Figure 7.29). The prices need to be realistic, so some research and common sense is required. (The child who bought an enormous amount, because every item cost only 1p, was quickly put right by the rest of the class.) This project provides the children with an enjoyable as well as a seasonal outcome to their learning.

Finally, the more able children are given the opportunity to use the spreadsheets to produce graphs showing the relative costs, and may even work with currency conversion formulae to see how their costs compare with those in other countries.[1]

Case study conclusion

Although the links with mathematics within this unit may appear tenuous at times, the school is sure that the ability to use and interpret data is a skill that is essential for many areas of mathematics. The school's policy is to encourage children to handle and interpret information from an early age, so that they are better able to face the increasing number of problem-solving activities required by the end of Key Stage 2. The use of relational databases is one such method.

Note

1   The authors make no apologies for including several case studies from one school. We wish to give examples of 'best practice', and accept it where we find it. We know there must be many schools who would fit this description, and we hope that when they read these case studies they will recognise much of what they themselves will be doing. For others who are just beginning to introduce this kind of work to their children, we trust these studies will give them practical help and encouragement.

Bibliography

Williams, J. and Easingwood, N., *ICT and Primary Science*, London, RoutledgeFalmer, 2003.

Chapter 8

Using graphs

It used to be said in the army, that if something moved you saluted it, and if it didn't you painted it – usually white. Since the general use of ICT in schools, this philosophy seems to have developed over the use of graphs. Perhaps because nearly every tool bar, of nearly every mathematics program, shows a 'graph' icon, teachers feel that they must use it. There are indeed many occasions when they should. However, teachers need to show their pupils, not only when to use graphs, but also which particular graph is the most appropriate for any given piece of information. The indiscriminate use of the wrong type of graph can give a misleading picture, or at the very least not show as much information as it should.

If we define a graph simply as a way of presenting or illustrating mathematical information (used in its widest sense), or sets of numbers, in such a way as to make them more easily understood, then we need to make sure that the graph we use does exactly that. Using graphs in the correct way can be great fun, and after producing lots of hard data, children are entitled to feel a sense of satisfaction when this is reproduced in graphical form at the click of a mouse. However, they do need to know why they are doing it, what the graph shows, if it shows the information in the correct way, and whether or not there is something else they should do to the graph, or whether that is the end of the process. It could actually be the beginning, for it is possible that the continued and automatic production of graphs, particularly if done within the confines of ICT 'lessons' rather than during active mathematics, may obscure the real use and nature of graphs. For older children, at least, the motivation brought about through the use of ICT should be utilised to rectify this. Although we have given the commonly used definition of a graph, we should better think of it as a diagram which shows a specific relationship between two sets of numbers and what they represent. Because each number comes alternatively from each set, then each pair is said to be 'ordered'.

Most graphs that children use will involve positive numbers. However, this of course will only use one quarter of a graph. It can be argued that we should show the complete graph, as illustrated by Figure 8.1, from an early age, even if the positive 'corner' is the only one used. The authors well remember how when they were first introduced to positive and negative axes used together on the same diagram, it took a long time for the penny to drop. Although well into secondary education, we were actually using the same graphs as we had always done. In pure mathematics, graphs may be used to illustrate (sometimes hitherto unknown) connections between sets of numbers, such as sequences of squared numbers, or to represent algebraic expressions. Since these hardly come within the domain of primary school mathematics, we will remain with our original definition of graphs as a pictorial representation of either simple data, or at least continual, and measurable, practical processes.

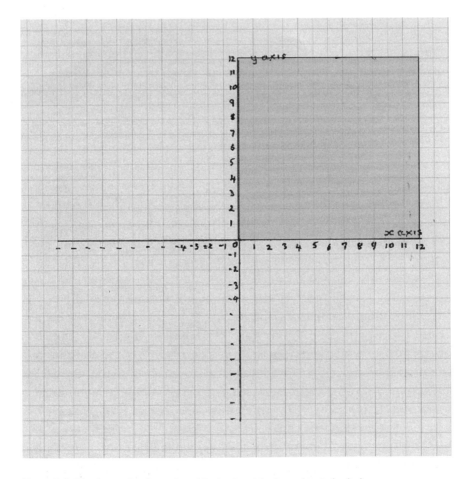

Figure 8.1 The 'complete' graph, with the 'positive' quadrant shaded.

Some examples of frequently used graphs and charts

Data can be displayed by bar charts, histograms and frequency diagrams, pictograms, pie charts and scatter graphs. Whilst most data can be displayed in more than one of these forms, each nevertheless has its unique purpose.

Bar charts

These show discrete sets of information, each represented by its own column or block. The monthly rainfall figures are a typical example of this type, as illustrated by Figure 8.2. The vertical axis gives the measurement of rain, whilst each block represents a month, and its length or height represents the amount of rain fallen. In a mathematics lesson, younger children may often draw these graphs to show the variety and numbers of pets owned by the class, or perhaps how each of them travels to school. With this kind of chart, although it is not essential, the numbers are usually on the vertical axis, whilst the sets of animals or methods of transport are on the horizontal.

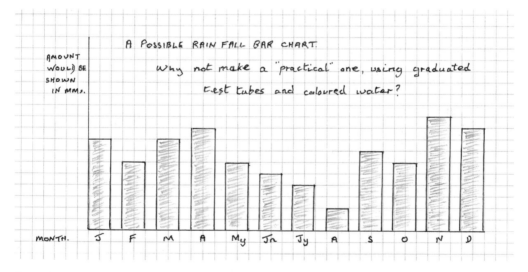

Figure 8.2 An example of a bar chart showing rainfall. Why not make a 'practical' one, using graduated test tubes and coloured water?

Histograms

These are special bar charts, where the frequency distribution is shown by the rectangles (bars), as illustrated by Figure 8.3. It should be drawn with these bars joined together, whereas in a simple bar graph they may have equal spaces between them. A typical histogram could be a graph showing the height of a group of primary-age children, with a predetermined group of heights – say every 10 cms – measured along the base line, with the shortest on the left. The number of children measured are listed at regular intervals. This would show the frequency (f), in other words how many children are in each 'height group'. Statisticians would probably expect a normal distribution with the largest group in the middle of the graph, and roughly the same number at each end. If the histogram does not fit this picture, then further research should find out why. This kind of graph is often used to measure the spread of marks in various tests and examinations. For instance, if a frequency distribution curve showing marks in a year's A-level results has a skew towards the higher marks, as illustrated by Figure 8.4, then it might suggest that pupils are working harder and being taught better. There again depending on your point of view (or if you are a politician out of government) you might think the examination is getting easier! The correct conclusion should of course depend on further research.

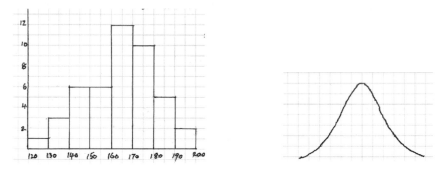

Figure 8.3 A histogram showing the heights of a group of 45 children. Data would have to be collected first, so that the range of heights can be decided. The children should fall within the ranges chosen. How close would the curve, if drawn on the histogram, come to the 'normal' curve shown on the right?

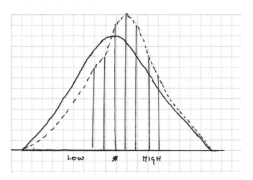

Figure 8.4 A line graph, or frequency polygon. The solid line is the normal distribution curve, as defined by algebra. The larger the sample, the nearer the histogram will match the precisely defined (mathematically) normal curve. In this example, if the curve followed the bars there would be a 'skew' towards the high end. The asterisk marks the expected mean average for the drawn normal distribution curve.

A line graph, sometimes called a frequency polygon, can be drawn by joining the mid points of the tops of the bars, as shown in Figure 8.4. This is a technique which we will use for other graphs later in this chapter.

Pictograms

These may superficially resemble bar charts, and are often used for such projects as traffic surveys. There are no scales involved, the total numbers of pictures often representing the actual numbers themselves. So, for example, if 10 children in the class walk to school, then 10 pictures of children will be used. Obviously, if the numbers are large, then one picture would need to represent a given number of children. For instance, one picture could represent five children, so with 10 children there would be two pictures. As long as this is clearly stated on the pictogram, it can prove an interesting teaching point. What, for instance, do you do if there are 14 children who walk to school? Perhaps two big pictures and four little ones.

Pie charts

These diagrams are a favourite with primary children, and are often part of many ICT programs. They are particularly useful when they need to illustrate units of time, whether it be an hour, a day or a year. Because it is based on a circle, and a circle 'has' 360 degrees, then the chart can be divided up into the correct proportions by measuring the degrees. Obviously this is done for the child by the computer, but for older children, at least, the idea that pie charts are based on degrees and proportionate fractions should be explained.

If the children were to measure their typical school day, they would need to first decide if it was to take in the complete 24 hours. This would be better both mathematically and because we should avoid emphasising that school is 'another place'. As long as they could use a protractor, the children could divide their circle into 24 equal parts, 15 degrees for each segment. Using a suitable program, the children could do this on the computer, either to complete the diagram electronically or to produce a blank printout to be completed by hand.

Because pie charts are used so widely, it is important for the children to make sure that they are used sensibly, if they are relevant, and whether the information could be shown in a better way. For example, if the pie chart shows only two sectors, one of which is often very small, is this really of much value?

They should be given the opportunity to click on the icon to see what the pie chart looks like, but need to understand that it might be a pointless exercise.

Scatter graph

This graph seems not to be used as often a bar or pie chart, which is a pity because it can give rise to some very interesting work. It may be that the program being used does not give this option, but even when it does the work being undertaken may not require the use of such a graph. When we use a scatter graph, we are, as in so many other aspects of mathematics, looking for a pattern. A scatter graph will show us if two very different sets of information have any connection. Often in science and mathematics they obviously do. We all know that if you plot a graph of the known diameters of circles in centimetres from, say, one to 10 on the horizontal axis, and measure and plot their circumferences on the vertical, it results in a series of points through which a straight line can be drawn. There is an obvious relationship between the diameter and circumference of all circles. Not all relationships are so obvious, nor should we jump to conclusions even if the graph shows a positive correlation. When certain illnesses are plotted against the geographical area in which they occur, it can often suggest that certain of these areas are in themselves dangerous places in which to live. However, after a closer look, it may be found that these places are ones of affluence or poverty, and it is in these factors and their corresponding effects on the inhabitants' diets, and not the place itself, which gives the true reason for the high incidence of illness. If the scatter of points is totally random we can decide that there is no correlation at all, whilst at other times there can be said to be a negative or inverse relationship. We would not expect there to be any relationship between the weights of children and their results in Standard Assessment Tests (SATS), although it would be interesting if there were. However, if we measured the intake of hot drinks by members of a class of children in the winter term, we might find that the intake increases as the weather gets colder. Since the temperature would be shown along the horizontal axis with lowest temperatures on the left, then the plots through which the line of best fit could be drawn would slant 'backwards', as illustrated by Figure 8.5.

Some of the more common projects in which scatter graphs could be used are the ones where measurements of the hands, feet, arm length and so on are collected. Any two of these can be collated, although it needs to be remembered that the children are still growing, and not all at the same rate. One of the best programs which allows for the use of a scatter graph is *Information Workshop*, which forms part of the *Black Cat Toolbox* from Granada Learning.

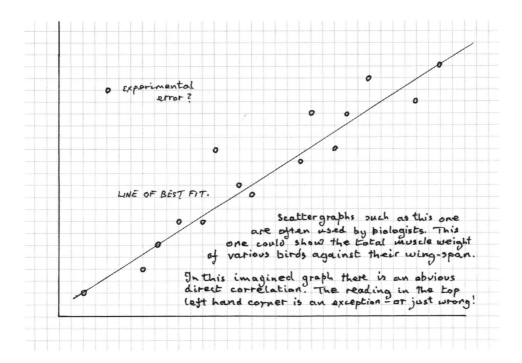

Figure within graph text:

o experimental
   error ?

LINE OF BEST FIT.

Scattergraphs such as this one
are often used by biologists. This
one could show the total muscle weight
of various birds against their wing-span.

In this imagined graph there is an obvious
direct correlation. The reading in the top
left hand corner is an exception – or just wrong!

Figure 8.5 A scattergraph showing the line of best fit.

It can be seen that a scatter graph can be a useful tool in any interesting project which involves comparing different and various factors. For a simple Key Stage 1 project, there might well be a correlation between the height of the various children in the class and the lengths of their arms or hand spans. We would not expect a correlation between height and eye or hair colour. However, both should be tried, as much can be learned from a negative. It is of course how the co-ordinates cluster that suggests whether there is a correlation or not. For some projects the co-ordinates will group together somewhere within the axes of the graph, for others there will be a more defined grouping along a diagonal. This is often found in ecological investigations, where there may be a connection between the vegetation of a given habitat and the populations of certain specific animals. The 'line of best fit', mentioned above, may be drawn from zero point to the opposite corner, but just as often it is a line drawn from the point nearest the zero to the co-ordinate point nearest to the furthest corner of the graph, as in Figure 8.5. A third possibility is one that can often show a very wide spread of co-ordinates, yet still have a slightly more dense cluster along a diagonal – a kind of half-way between the first two. This can occur when a large number of plots are made between two factors that may have a connection, albeit a rather vague one. A good example of this kind occurs where the marks in tests are compared. Is there a correlation between the marks in say, English and maths?

Most people tend to be good at both (to start with at any rate), but by no means all.

The children should be encouraged to draw conclusions from the scatter graph, whatever it shows. They could be asked various questions, such as:
- 'Are all the points in one place?'

If they are then:
- 'Why do you think they are?'
- 'What do you think that means? Remember, what are we trying to measure/show?'

If they are not, then:
- 'Why do you think the points are all over the place?'
- 'What do you think this tells us?'
- 'Do you think it helps us very much?'
- 'Is there another kind of graph that will show this better?'

When they have studied their graphs, they may well come to some conclusions that may need further testing. It is hoped that they would be given this opportunity.

Line graphs

This is a very general term, and is often used to differentiate any graph from the standard block graph. It is a term that should be used with caution, as many things in mathematics, from algebraic equations to logarithms, parabolas and even musical scales, can be shown in graphic form, which range from straight lines to gentle curves. Most of these are beyond the scope of primary school children, although one of the authors' Year 6 class did build a parabolic reflector, having first drawn the template by plotting 1, 2, 3, etc. on the x axis against the square of that number (1, 4, 9, etc.) on the y axis. The children had no difficulty with drawing this graph, and most found it a useful reinforcement and a motivation for remembering their multiplication tables. One thing children need to remember is that a thin bar chart is not a line graph.

We often need to use a line graph when we are showing a continuous operation such as a temperature graph (human or geographical) or a graph to show the growth of a plant. Although temperatures may stay constant at various times, and plants may slow their growth for one reason or another, such as draught or cold weather, it is nevertheless a continuous process and needs to be shown as such. If, for example the growth of a plant or the air temperature are shown on a block graph, with the readings taken at a particular time of the day, what happens in between? The temperature can fluctuate considerably within one day, and unless there are going to be several blocks drawn for each day, we shall never know. However, if children plot a few points, and then join them up, we not only have a convenient method of showing what happens all the time, but the graph will also give us a clear picture from which the children can make predictions and draw conclusions. In the case of the plant graph, we also have the problem in schools of what happens at weekends. Although this applies to some extent to the temperature graph as well, with the growth of a plant, children may find a considerable difference between the measurements taken on Fridays and those taken on Mondays. It need not matter too much, but by using a continuous line we can at least estimate what the height of the plant was on the Saturday and Sunday. There are many good programs that allow children to plot the growth of a plant. One of the most easy to use is *Number Box*, a spreadsheet package that forms part of the *Black Cat Toolbox* from Granada Learning (see Figure 8.6). Although this, like many other simple programs, only enables children to produce a block graph, this can be overcome by simply

Growing a Plant

Date	Height	Height Increase
20/10/03	10.00	0.00
21/10/03	10.80	0.80
22/10/03	11.20	0.40
23/10/03	11.90	0.70
24/10/03	12.50	0.60
25/10/03		-12.50
26/10/03		
27/10/03	14.80	14.80
28/10/03	16.00	1.20
29/10/03	17.10	1.10

Figure 8.6 A screenshot from the *Number Box Quick Sheet* option for *Growing a Plant*. The authors have imagined that they are children recording the growth of a plant on a daily basis. Note, however, that the measurements could not be taken on the 25th and 26th as this was the weekend. The negative number has appeared in the height increase column because the formula in the spreadsheet has been set up to subtract a given height from the height recorded on the previous day. As there is no reading for the 25th, it has subtracted the previous day's reading from 0, hence a reading of –12.50. This in turn has affected the graph illustrated in Figure 8.7. Clearly the plant has not moved 12.5 cms in the other direction, so this is a misconception that will need to be clarified and explained as a teaching point.

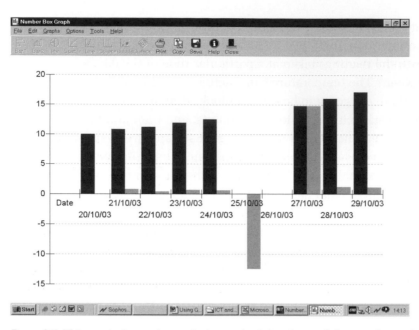

Figure 8.7 This graph shows the gradual growth of the plant and the gap shows the weekend where no measurements could be taken. Note the negative bar, caused by the 'mistake' in the spreadsheet shown in Figure 8.6. This can be ignored.

joining up the top points of the blocks on the print-out with a pencil, similar to the lines drawn at the top of the blocks in Figure 8.4. At the same time the dates and the weekend 'gap' can be allowed for.

Stereograms

These are in effect three-dimensional histograms and used to be made as a class activity out of blocks laid on a flat paper grid which in fact is nothing but a two-dimensional graph with 'vertical' and 'horizontal' axes. It was usual to exhibit the height and weight groups within a class or year group in this way. Each block would contain the number of children within each group, say those whose height was between 120 and 130 cms and whose weight fell into a suitable measurable group in kilograms. There might well be several children who fit into the height group, but who also fit into several different weight groups, or conversely whose height differs significantly but who fit into the same height group. A stereogram can show this clearly.

There are several programs which give simple 3-D interpretations of histograms, although these are not necessarily the same as stereograms. It is an ideal project for the computer, although a more sophisticated spreadsheet package, such as

Microsoft Excel, would need to be used. This surely would give added value to the use of ICT, for we can no longer imagine (sadly) that teachers have the time to produce the model described in the paragraph above.

Data logging

This application, which we have described at length in our book *ICT and Primary Science*, allows for the automatic collection and analysis of data through a range of sensors attached to the computer via a control box. The data are also displayed in a series of graphs, often shown together on one display. There are a variety of sensors which can monitor such variables as the temperature, light intensity and sound. All these can be displayed in graphical form (see Figure 8.8: the sound pattern is the jagged line shown on the screen of an oscilloscope), so as to give an overall picture of the conditions, over a given time, of any habitat, be it an ecological environment or the children's classroom.

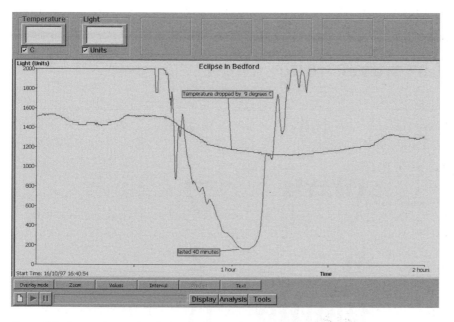

Figure 8.8 A typical sample of the graphical information obtained from sensors during a data logging project (reproduced by kind permission of Data Harvest Limited).

Case study: a class travel survey

Our thanks to Jan Yates and her Year 1 class at Letchmore Infants and Nursery School, Stevenage, Hertfordshire for this study, which illustrates how various graphs can be used even by the youngest children.

The teacher introduced this topic to the children by suggesting that they find out how they all travelled to school and what the most popular method was. During this initial stage they discovered that there were four ways: by car, bus, bicycle and on foot. This information was entered onto a tally chart by the teacher. Each child then entered their mark on this chart against the correct heading (see Figure 8.9) and as they did so collected the appropriate picture and fixed it to the class graph (Figure 8.10). This involved considerable class discussion about how best to produce a graph, which kind was the clearest and how the information that they had already collected could most clearly be presented.

The children were then introduced to the idea of using a computer program to display and collate their work. Again considerable discussion took place in the

Our travel tally chart

The way we travel to school.	tally	total
walk	††††††	7
bus	††	2
car	†††††††† †	11
bicycle	†	1

Figure 8.9 Recording the information on a chart prepared for the children by the teacher.

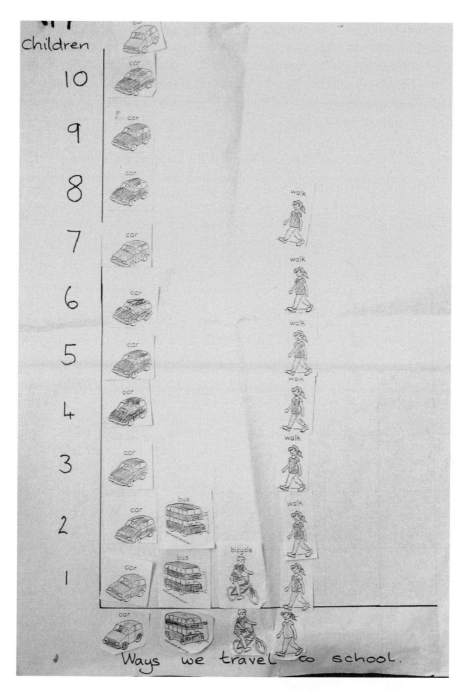

Figure 8.10 The pictogram on the classroom wall. Each child had the opportunity to select their own mode of transport, colour an individual picture and stick it on to the class graph.

school's computer room over the benefits of computer-generated graphs and how these would enable the children to analyse the figures and reproduce them in a variety of different graphical representations. Using the *RM Starting Graph* program all the children individually entered the data from the class graph onto the school's computers, so that each child could produce relevant graphs and charts (see Figures 8.11 to 8.13).

Although this small project was designed to fulfil the requirements of the Numeracy Hour, and did so very well, the subsequent use of ICT brought a new

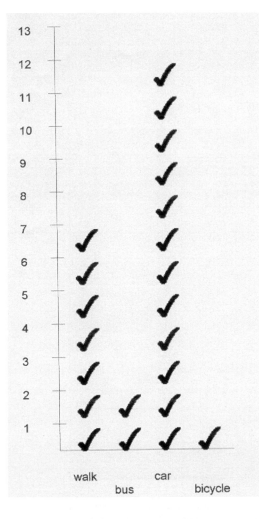

Figure 8.11 Some children used a blank outline graph in combination with their own felt-tipped pens to record their data.

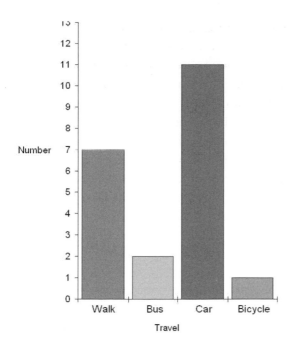

Figure 8.12 Other children used the graphing function of *RM Starting Graph*.

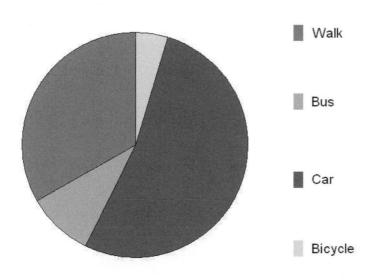

Figure 8.13 The children also looked to see if a pie chart would show the information as clearly as the graphs. They soon realised that their version did not include numbers and therefore did not give a sufficient amount of information.

dimension to the work. There are several other points that should be emphasised:

- The children used their own computer work in order to show the most and least popular methods of transport, and to discover how many children used one method rather than another.
- The raw data were originally collected and collated by the children themselves, with appropriate help from their teacher.
- There was always considerable and relevant class discussion at each stage.
- All the class used the computers, all attained a high level of keyboard skills, and the majority of the children were very able independently to manipulate and analyse the data.

Bibliography

Williams, J., 'Building solar furnaces: an example of science in the primary school', *School Science Review, Journal of the ASE*, 223(December), 1981: 267–76.

Chapter 9

Mathematics across the curriculum

Mathematics has been described as the queen of subjects, whilst also being the servant to others, which is one reason why we refer to the cross-curricular approach to teaching at various times in this book. This is of course far from new, but unfortunately it appears not to be in fashion at the moment. Nevertheless, it is advocated in the National Curriculum, and various opportunities to use this approach are even highlighted. But it does not appear in the programmes written for the National Numeracy Strategy. This is one of those contradictions that we have mentioned before. However, if you read the background information to the Numeracy Strategy, you find that it stresses the need to look for opportunities to draw mathematical experiences from a wide range of activities. If this means that teachers need to look for cross-curricular activities, then it would surely be a help if the programmes indicated where these can be found. The National Curriculum does do this, and so might the new 'Primary School Curriculum', which at the time of writing is in the first stages of development.

When a cross-curricular approach was in vogue, it was perhaps much closer to both actual everyday living, and to real learning, than the more structured timetable-led approach. Indeed it could be suggested that as advanced 'grown-up' learning had to be cross-curricular in order to work, primary school children came closer to real learning than at any other time before they reached adulthood. If there is even a grain of truth in this argument, then this is another good reason for favouring this approach, at least for part of the school day. Another consideration is that it seems to make good sense not to create artificial subject boundaries either in the actual timetable or in the minds of the learner.

The National Curriculum document for mathematics lists several opportunities to make links to other subjects, notably ICT and English. Teachers should be prepared to foster these links, and indeed try to take every opportunity to widen them, and include work on graphics and science as well as the arts and the humanities. Most of the work in this chapter will also fit very well into sections of the Numeracy Strategy programmes, such as space and shape, and solving problems.

Science

There are many and obvious connections between science and mathematics. We have discussed many of them in our book *ICT and Primary Science* (Williams and Easingwood, 2003). However, much of this deals with the mathematics needed to help explain and record the results of scientific experimentation. However, in this chapter we are in fact looking more at the mathematics that is often taught in more conventional ways, but might be better explained if a less obvious route is followed: for example, using genuine mathematics within other subjects to teach necessary mathematical skills and concepts. This is very similar to the work on surface area and volume described in Chapter 7, 'Handling data'.

Despite the more seemingly structured approach of the National Curriculum and the Numeracy Strategy programmes, there are nevertheless examples of cross-curricular materials still being published. One recent example is the 'Science and Plants in Schools' (SAPS) project. This includes several examples of how plants can be used to enhance children's mathematics learning. It even suggests a range of activities that can enliven the 10 minutes' mental arithmetic that begins the numeracy hour. One of the SAPS topics suggests that children make pictograms of a collection of holly leaves to show the number of spines, with the base scale indicating the various numbers of the spines. By so doing, children can not only begin to understand the biological significance of the variations of leaf, but can enhance their mathematical knowledge of such things as measurement and averages. Whilst this can be done by making the pictogram with the actual leaves, there is a great opportunity to utilise the properties of the computer for counting and data analysis, as well as for actually drawing the pictograms.

Another area of science that lends itself to ICT, and particularly to the use of the interactive whiteboard, is the study of food chains. This is an important section of the National Curriculum, to be found in 'Living Things and their Environment', at Key Stage 2. Food chains are relatively simple to understand, but not easy for primary school children to study as a practical project, as it is almost impossible to isolate a chain of animals, from herbivores eating grass, leaves or seeds, through to primary and secondary carnivores. However, it is important for children to be given opportunities for 'minds-on' activities as well as 'hands-on' ones (Dorothy Watt, 1999). One possible method of explaining a food chain is to list as many animals as the children can name. This is where the interactive whiteboard comes into its own. Using their own (and the teacher's) general knowledge, they can decide where a selection of animals fit into a food chain, which animals feed on others, or whether they are mainly or totally a herbivore. Link them together with appropriate arrows. The teacher will likely as not find that there are many cross-linkages, so that the chain becomes a more complex, and realistic, food web. The mathematics in these chains lies in the sequencing of the design, which in some ways is similar to a flowchart. However, teachers need to be aware that a biologist usually calculates the food chain as a flow of energy. The 'biomass' of each stage is measured mathematically, and built up step by step as a graphical pyramid. Plant life of whatever kind will form the base, and must of course have the largest biomass.

Graphics

Teachers may wonder why we include 'graphics' in a book about mathematics, forming, as it does, a part of the design element of the technology curriculum. The authors feel that there is a genuine and not contrived connection, particularly when ICT is also involved. There used to be a subject called 'technical drawing'. Whatever the limitations this subject may have had, it did at least include much basic geometry such as shapes, parallels and angles. To some extent many of these are still part of any graphics work, and would be relevant for much of the work in the 'Measures, Shape and Space' sections of the Numeracy Strategy. For example, children often need to draw three-dimensional shapes. Mostly these are cubes or cuboids, but there is no reason why this drawing should not extend to other simple shapes, such as a cylinder. When a cube is drawn using the actual measurements we will have an accurate mathematical representation, although to the eye it will look 'crooked', or at least not aesthetically pleasing. This may be a good time to cross the boundaries and introduce the children to the idea of perspective. This does not mean we leave mathematics behind: shapes are shapes however they are drawn, and still require measurement, parallels and angles. Figures 9.1, 9.2 and 9.3 show how a cubic shape can be drawn using one- and two-point perspective. Figure 9.4 illustrates the drawing of a cylinder, for which a new shape is introduced. In a perspective drawing the front of the cylinder needs to be drawn as an ellipse. It is best to use a template for this.

The authors have found that most children in Years 5 and 6 can cope with this very well. It is a good idea, when introducing them to perspective drawing, to

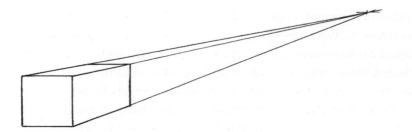

Figure 9.1 A drawing using single-point perspective.

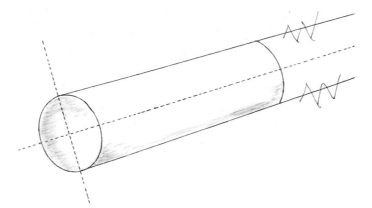

Figure 9.2 A drawing using two-point perspective. All vertical lines in this drawing and the one above need to be parallel.

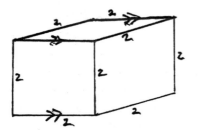

Figure 9.3 A mathematically correct cube.

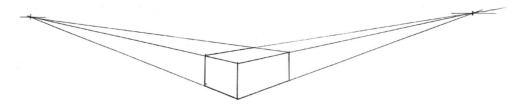

Figure 9.4 The mathematics of a perspective drawing: the shape of a cylinder. The dotted lines are the x and y axes around which the shape is drawn, with an ellipse at the front to replicate the circular end (try drawing a circle and see what it looks like). The lines of perspective might meet at the far corner of the board – they are of course rubbed out later. A little shading completes the picture.

stand them at the end of a long corridor and suggest that they place their hands in front of their face (not over their eyes), and ask them if they can see the far wall. They should not be able to see it. Now ask them to explain why not – their hand is certainly not bigger than the distant wall. Draw their attention to the way that the walls and ceiling seem to converge on this distant wall – in particular, how the 'lines' that form the corners of the corridor converge. Are they able to explain this? After children have had practice at this kind of drawing, it is interesting to observe how they use this knowledge in other ways. We have found that they no longer complain that their drawings of houses are 'too flat', and their drawings of things like trees become more realistic. They can now either accept this 'flatness', or they can try to draw a perspective view. In their art work they should of course be allowed to take artistic license when appropriate. 'Flat' houses are fine if that is what they want, but now they at least have the choice.

Moreover, we have noticed that children often view their immediate world in an altogether different way once they grasp the concept of perspective. We discovered a very simple example quite by chance. A child had drawn a pair of spectacles with the ear pieces sticking out in a straight line from both sides of the lenses. She was not happy with this, so her sister, who had had lessons on perspective at another school, pointed out that the ear pieces should have been drawn parallel to each other, and behind the lenses. The first child may have drawn the spectacles in this way eventually anyway, but her satisfaction and interest in this new way of drawing simple things was very clear to see. Perhaps this is a lesson on when it is appropriate for the teacher to introduce a new idea. We have already seen in Chapter 3 that the use of an interactive whiteboard can further enhance the teaching of this particular mathematical topic. Figure 3.13 illustrated a three-dimensional cube drawn on a tile of isometric graph paper on the board. The teacher can draw the cube edge by edge, explaining how the three-dimensional shape is drawn in two dimensions. The use of the interactive whiteboard allows this visual representation to be produced step by step, accurately and neatly. Children can then come up and use the board for themselves, perhaps applying the same principle to extend the cube to other shapes such as a cuboid. This is illustrated by Figure 9.5 overleaf.

Art and design

Like graphics, art at first sight may seem to have no connection with mathematics or ICT. Of course it need not, for the authors are certainly not advocating painting by numbers, and colour, texture and the actual subject of the painting can all be appreciated for their own sakes. That is obviously what

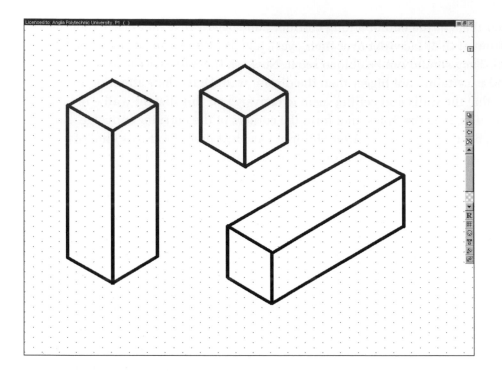

Figure 9.5 Mathematically accurate drawings produced on the interactive whiteboard. The teacher has produced a cube, followed by two cuboids in different positions. When drawn line by line using the annotation tool, the teacher is able to produce shapes that are accurate and which illustrate carefully how these should be drawn. Note that these are not perspective drawings.

we hope children will be able to do, but there are nevertheless good reasons for teachers to view paintings at least for the opportunities they offer to help motivate children to become interested in other areas of the curriculum. Science teaching can obviously be enhanced by a study of certain painters. Most notably, perhaps, Joseph Wright (of Derby) who painted many scientific and industrial subjects, although there are others less obvious. Nor is it necessary to visit a gallery to see these. Many can be viewed using CD-ROMs, or better still on various gallery Websites.

Many paintings apparently show no mathematical connections whatsoever. However, it may lie hidden in the very composition of the picture, for the artist may have organised or chosen the subject in such a way as to give a certain balance to the composition. This is most obvious when certain aspects of subjects allied to art such as architecture are considered. There is a particular mathematical proportion, the so-called 'Golden Section', which was well known to the original Greeks who have left us with many fine examples in their ancient buildings. It has been often incorporated in the design of much architecture, and in many paintings. Mathematically we need to think of the section as a rectangle constructed so that its height (h) and its width (w) are in the proportion:

$$\frac{w}{h} = \frac{h}{w+h}$$

There are, however, many paintings that show obvious mathematical connections. These are often found within collections of so-called 'modern art', and the whole of the cubist movement might well be included within this description. Beauty (or art) may well be in the eye of the beholder, but unless you belong to the 'I know what I like, and only like what I know' school of art critic, then these can be viewed with at least an open mind. This is after all what we would want our children to do. Many such paintings are pure geometry, and it would be interesting for the children to take measurements, and look to see if there is an underlying numerical pattern. Figures 9.6 to 9.11 show some examples of art very closely allied to a mathematical structure. Many teachers will recognise the sculptures as based on mathematical nets similar to those drawn for simple cubic shapes.

Nets as finished sculptures in three dimensions made by artist Liz Ballard, exhibited in Paris in 2002

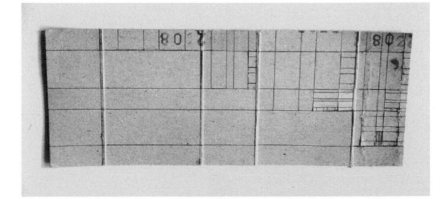

Figure 9.6 Step One: the net is drawn onto a piece of card.

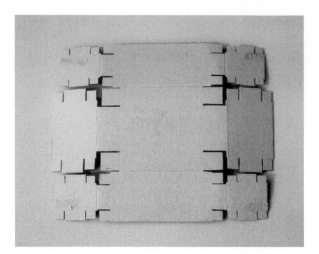

Figure 9.7 Step Two: the net is cut out and scored ready for folding.

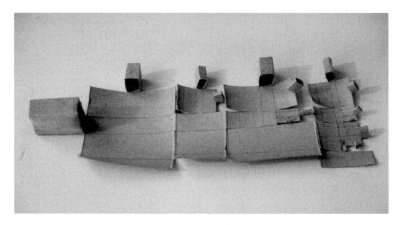

Figure 9.8 Step Three: the first folds are made.

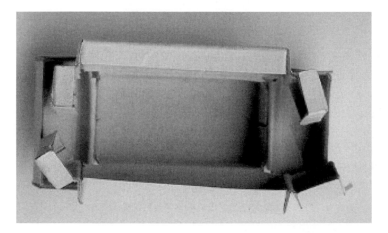

Figure 9.9. A photograph of the net as a finished sculpture in three dimensions made by Liz Ballard.

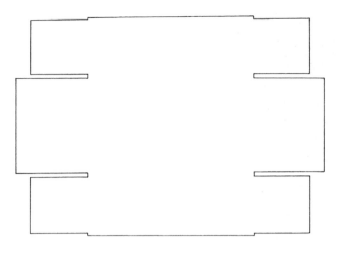

Figure 9.10 A net of the sculpture in Figure 9.9.

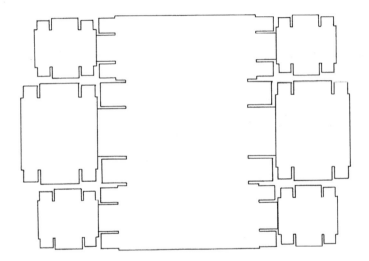

Figure 9.11 A net of the sculpture with the folds cut out.

Figures 9.12 to 9.17 show the development of this mathematical idea with one drawing carrying on from each of the previous ones to create a kind of fractal in two dimensions, just as the nets in Figure 9.6, 9.7 and 9.8 show these in three-dimensional form. These drawings are based on the outside net for the matchbox sculptures. The artist, Liz Ballard, describes these as 'Each subsequent drawing shows Fractals either decreasing or increasing' (note: not all the drawings can be shown here. Readers might like to imagine what the other drawings could look like).

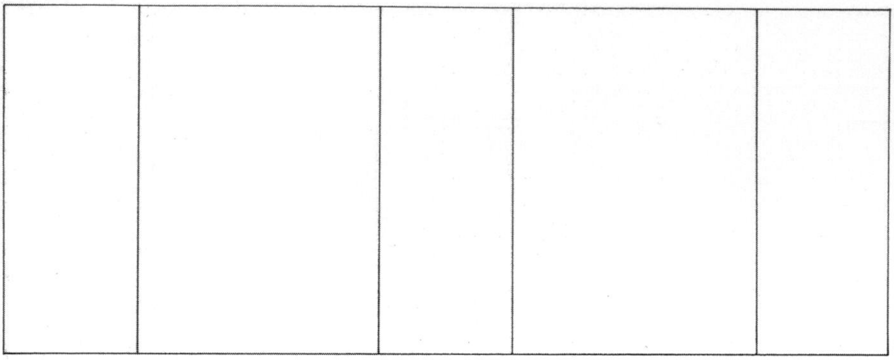

Figure 9.12 Step One.

Figure 9.13 Step Two.

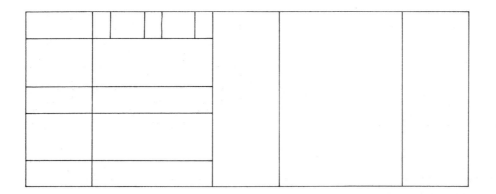

Figure 9.14 Step three.

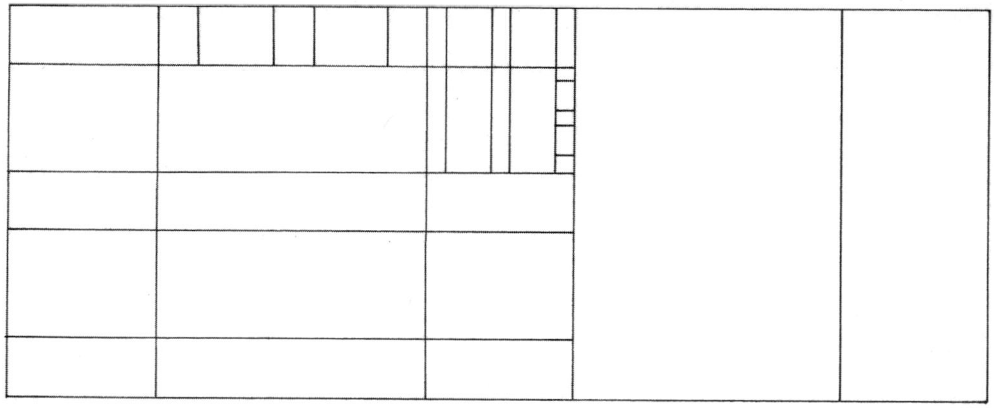

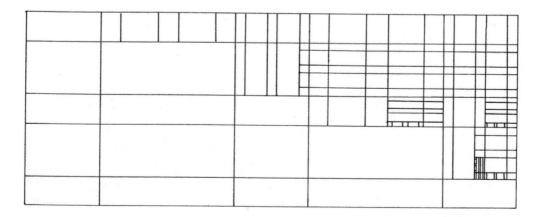

Figure 9.15 Step Four.

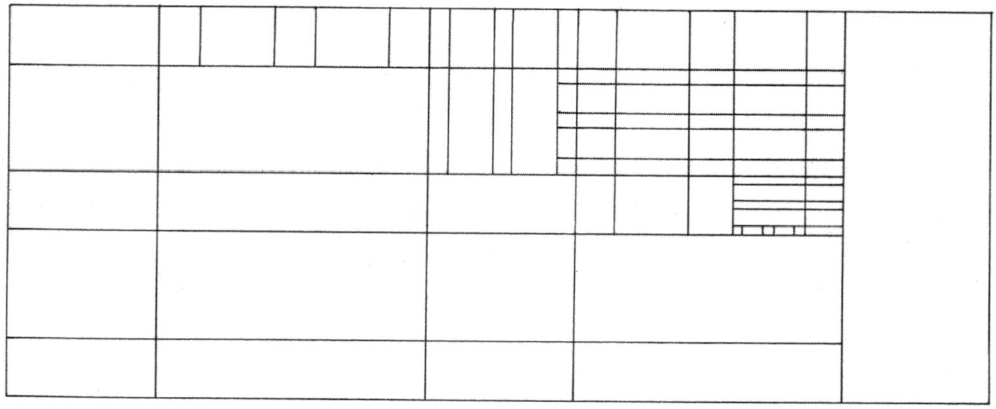

Figure 9.16 Step Five.

Figure 9.17 Step Six.

Fractals in art

These are really 'New Mathematics' and are a form of geometry based on similar shapes. In geometry 'similar' means the same shape, and in the same proportion; it does not have to mean the same size. Because of these properties, fractals can increase or decrease in size an infinite number of times. They are rather like the problem of the frog that always jumps half the distance across a pond. His first jump takes him halfway across, his second jump, half of the remaining distance again, and so on. Does he ever get to the other side? Obviously at the moment Fractals are beyond the scope of primary mathematics. However, as the drawings above show, with the appropriate use of a simple drawing package some of the basic ideas need not be. If readers wish to find out more about Fractals, the latest developments in this field can be found on the Web at: http://math.rice.edu/~lanius/fractals/.

Figure 9.18 shows a perspective drawing, highly mathematical in its use of shape. It is a drawing based on the numerous small exhibition bays in the main hall the 'Salle des Fêtes' de St Hélène in France, and actually represents a 360-degree view as seen from one central point. Apart from the drawing of the mathematical shapes themselves, this idea can easily be used by children for a variety of graphical representations with the use of a digital camera and simple panorama software, which can be downloaded for free from the Internet. Children can record any number of 'all-round' pictures by simply standing in one place, pointing the camera at a particular object, or better still another child, and turning a full circle, capturing images every 30 degrees or so. Care must be taken to ensure that the images 'match' each other by being at the same level, and some overlap must occur for the images to be electronically 'stitched' together. The resulting image is displayed as a panorama, where the user can use the mouse to rotate the images as one continuous scene, giving the impression that the user is standing in the middle of a room or landscape. The more sophisticated pieces of spin panorama software allow the user to zoom in or out and up and down. This feature is commonly used on the Websites of museums and art galleries to enable the user to go on 'virtual tours' of their exhibits. At a more basic level, the resulting image can be inserted into a document that has the object, or child, pictured at both ends. Figure 9.19 illustrates this. (It is rather like the school photograph belonging to one of the authors, where one pupil appears at both ends, for he had run behind the rows of standing children whilst the camera slowly panned round on its moveable tripod – technology can sometimes take the fun out of life.) As Millwood (2000) states, the whole process of capturing the images, downloading them to a computer and stitching them together can take as little as 15 minutes. Even quite young children are capable of managing this

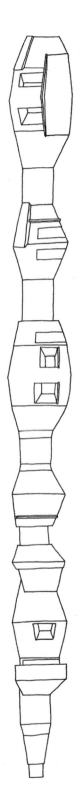

Figure 9.18 Perspective drawing of the 'Salle des Fêtes' de St Hélène, France. Liz Ballard (2002/3).

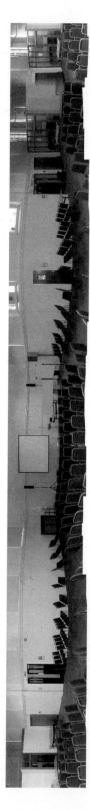

Figure 9.19 An example of a panorama. This is one of the lecture theatres at Anglia Polytechnic University in Chelmsford. One of the authors produced this continuous image by standing amongst the chairs in the middle of the room, and then taking 19 separate images using a digital camera. Care was taken to ensure that there was some overlap between each image, and that each shot was of the same elevation. He then downloaded some free 'stitching' software from the Internet and loaded the separate images into it. A 'wizard' then did the rest. There were options to present the finished panorama as one image, as illustrated here, or as a continuous image for display on a Web page. The whole process took less than 10 minutes. (Courtesy: www.panoramafactory.com)

process. Millwood goes on to say that this is an interactive medium that allows the user to navigate what is not a fixed, pictorial composition as used in conventional still photography, but a whole scene.

The computer as a medium for art and mathematics

Children can be encouraged to produce their own drawings using ICT-based art software packages. The work of painters such as Mondrian allows a picture to be created using a series of parallel lines and regular squares and rectangles, some of which are filled by colour. Children can then create their own versions of work by famous artists that encourage them to think about the properties of shapes and space, and how they relate to each other. This could be developed into work involving tessellations, whereby the same shape can be reproduced and fitted together on the screen. Most art packages come complete with tools for producing a range of regular shapes, and paint tools to fill them with colour. Whilst there is no substitute for children actually fitting 'real' shapes made of cardboard or plastic together, the use of ICT enables the child to produce patterns quickly, easily and neatly – and above all accurately and consistently, an essential aspect when exploring key aspects of space and shape such as tessellations. As we have already discussed in Chapter 3, which concerns the use of the interactive whiteboard, the facility exists within most graphics packages to allow 'rubber banding' whereby pupils can click on a shape in the shape tool menu, and then drag it and transform it into different proportions and positions (see Figure 9.20).

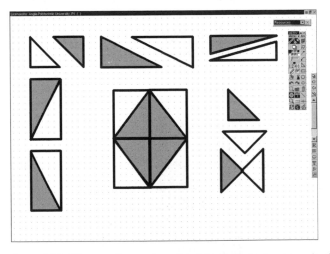

Figure 9.20 The transformation of a right-angled triangle as displayed on the Promethean *Activboard*. The first triangle drawn is in the top left-hand corner of the screen. This original has been transformed by 'rubber banding', a technique similar to using elastic bands on a pin or peg board, as frequently found in Key Stage 1 classrooms.

This can be further developed through the use of more sophisticated transformation tools within the package, including:

- Rotation tools: Allowing the shape to be rotated through a given number of degrees – usually 45 and 90 degrees, but more advanced packages allow rotation through any number of degrees. This is especially useful when illustrating to younger children that one shape can be moved into any position without any of the properties changing.
- Mirror tools: Allowing the mirroring of shapes along the x or y axes. This is particularly useful for symmetry and, when used with the rotate tool detailed above, rotational symmetry (usually taught at the top end of Key Stage 2).
- Flip tools: Allowing the flipping of shapes in the x or y axes;
- Duplication tools: Allowing any number of the shapes to be copied and then put into new positions to give a repeating pattern, giving a similar response to repeats or procedures in LOGO.

These features look particularly impressive when used on an interactive whiteboard, as the children can see the shapes being transformed in front of their very eyes, or even experiment with transforming shape themselves. However, they can engage in this activity even where no whiteboard is available. *Microsoft Office* applications such as *Word* and *PowerPoint* both contain drawing tools which are sufficiently sophisticated for primary age children. These can be selected from the 'Toolbars' option in the 'View' menu, and the drawing toolbar appears just above the taskbar at the bottom of the screen. The children can work individually or in pairs on the computer, or, if they have access to a data projector, they can present their findings to the rest of the class by controlling the mouse and projecting the images to a board in the 'old-fashioned' way. As with the *Activboard* software, a wide range of shapes can be selected and arranged on the page. They can be filled with different colours and labelled using a text box. One more advanced and very useful feature is the (three-dimensional) '3-D' tool, which is the icon at the extreme right-hand end of the drawing toolbar. Two-dimensional (2-D) shapes can be drawn onto the screen, and can be filled to give the impression of a solid shape. When the '3-D' button is pressed, another series of options appear which, when individually selected, transform the 2-D shape in a number of different ways to give the impression of being in three dimensions. A particularly useful and impressive feature is the '3-D' settings toolbar, where the shapes can be rotated in different planes when clicking on a button. Figures 9.21 to 9.23 illustrate this feature. Figure 9.24 illustrates where the shape has been changed from 'solid' to 'wire frame' appearance, particularly useful when explaining the properties of three-dimensional shapes to children.

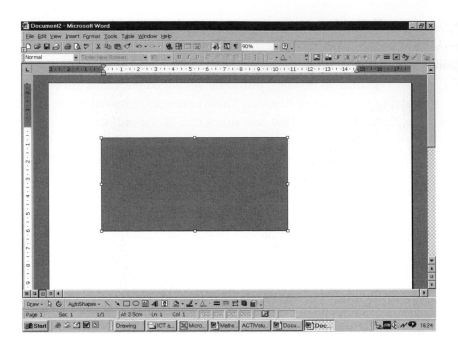

Figure 9.21 Step One: rotating a three-dimensional shape in *Microsoft Word*. A shape is drawn on the page and is filled. Note the drawing toolbar near the bottom of the screen.

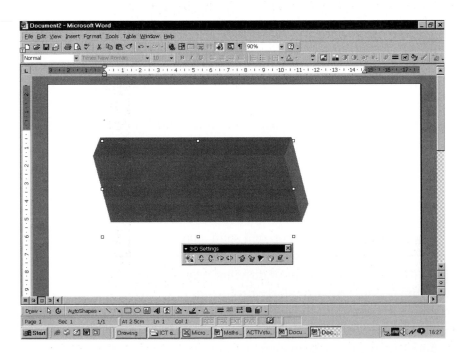

Figure 9.22 Step Two: using the '3-D' settings option, the shape takes on the appearance of having three dimensions, and is then tilted downwards. Note the 'floating toolbar' which is accessed by clicking the '3-D' button at the right-hand end of the drawing toolbar.

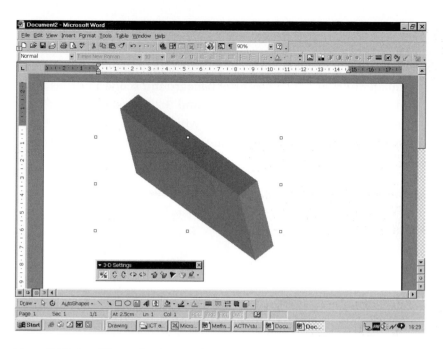

Figure 9.23 Step Three: the shape is then tilted to the left.

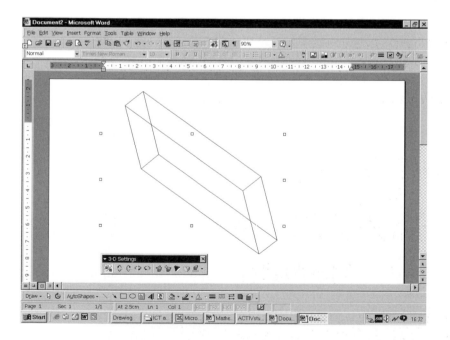

Figure 9.24 By clicking on the 'surface' tool (second button from the right on the '3-D' settings floating toolbar) the shape can be changed to 'wire frame' mode. This is useful for demonstrating to children what happens to 'invisible' surfaces when a shape is moved into a different position. This is selected by clicking the 'Surface' button, second from right on the '3-D' settings toolbar.

This work can then be developed into more complex graphics work involving shapes and images. It could mimic the work of Escher, a mathematician who explored the use of repeating similar shapes to produce new patterns, including optical illusions. Imaginative use of some of the background scenes, or tiles, can further extend and enhance this idea. Figures 9.25 and 9.26 illustrate this. The user begins by selecting a suitable background tile which readily lends itself to transformation or rotation. In this example we have used the 'Flag' option from the tile backgrounds in the 'Fun' menu.

Figure 9.25 Background tile of a repeating image of a flag.

By clicking on the 'Camera' option from the main menu, and selecting the 'Area Snapshot' option, the user can 'photograph' a given area of the background by dragging the mouse over the required tiles, in this case one of the flags. The right-hand mouse button is then clicked and the option 'To current flipchart page' selected. This opens a further menu which allows the user to transform the selected area in a number of ways. This is illustrated by Figure 9.26.

A larger area can also be selected. Figure 9.27 illustrates where four flags have been selected and transformed by being mirrored and then rotated through 90 degrees.

Figure 9.26 Background tile of flags with the central flag rotated through 180 degrees. This effect can also be achieved by using the flip or mirror options in the x or y axes.

Figure 9.27 Four flags have been selected, then mirrored and rotated to give a different image.

There are of course many different permutations that can be employed in order to address several key mathematical topics. By using the 'Rotate', 'Mirror' and 'Flip' tools, the teacher can use the interactive whiteboard to support areas of learning such as symmetry, rotational symmetry, shape and space and area. The teacher can demonstrate to the children step by step how shapes can be selected and transformed in several different ways. The children can also use the board themselves to experiment with the different functions to attempt to achieve similar effects, as well as to model the construction of quite complex patterns. Some interesting Escher-like pictures could be produced, where regular shapes could be transformed in many different ways and the images themselves changed. The resulting images, although clearly mathematical, could produce some very impressive and innovative artwork.

Other areas of the curriculum

If you look hard enough you can probably find mathematics in virtually every subject. You could certainly incorporate ICT into them. However, we do not wish to labour the mathematical point too much, although there is certainly a need for the ICT element to be considered. Nevertheless, as far as this volume is concerned we should at least briefly consider three further subjects, geography, history, and physical education (PE).

Geography

We have already suggested how the results of geographical projects such as recording and analysing rainfall, temperature, and other general weather conditions (handling data), can be enhanced by the good use of ICT, as well as the links to direction and distance (floor turtle and LOGO). One particularly mathematical area that also lends itself to the imaginative use of ICT in certain well-defined circumstances is the study and drawing of compass bearings. Figure 9.28 shows a simple picture that could have been drawn by many children, either on paper or on the computer screen. On it are superimposed the bearings and angles to and from the various points. This is of course how sailors use charts or, with a third bearing, how maps are drawn, although scale and distance must also be considered for an accurate representation. The original drawing can be imaginary, although if possible an actual site, perhaps the classroom or playground, should be used. Indeed, the authors would not wish for ICT to be used where it would be more appropriate for the children to actually carry out a practical study, be it in art, science or any other subject. If we are not careful we could be in danger of finding ourselves teaching subjects like music, without the children touching a musical instrument, although computers can in certain circumstances allow young children to develop a creative interest in music (Richard Ager, 1998). So, whilst keeping all this in mind, we suggest that certain of these projects could come under the title of a 'Special Activity', perhaps because it is beyond the scope of practicality, such as food chains, or simply because it is raining outside. Drawing bearings as described above could be one such activity, as could the switch circuitry described in Chapter 5. Recording, where appropriate, is another matter and can always be done on a computer. For example, spreadsheets could show very clearly, in one column, a list of the bearings from the set points to some 'treasure' on the playground (Figure 9.28). In another column, the children could list the reciprocal bearings from the treasure to the fixed point. It would be an

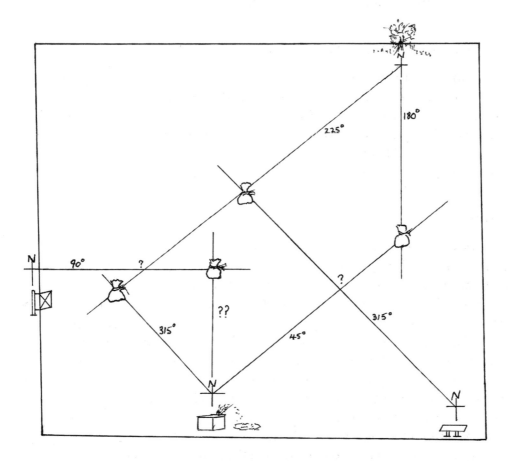

Figure 9.28 Finding bags of treasure in the playground. A drawing of a playground with five particular landmarks, each with their respective bearings drawn in. Bearings are taken from these known objects, in this case from bush and bench, then from bush and twice from the drinking fountain, and then from the gate and a third from the fountain. We have only used angles that are familiar compass bearings. The question marks are 'teaching points' for the children to answer, i.e. what are the reciprocal bearings? Need there be treasures where every bearing crosses?

interesting mathematical challenge for children to think how these reciprocal bearings could be calculated.

History

There may be particular aspects of history such as a study of the development of clocks, or the history of numbers, that lend themselves to mathematics and or ICT. However, we often consider history is a kind of 'time study' in itself. When the teacher constructs a time line in the classroom, it is not, one hopes, to expect the children to learn all the dates, but to put the events in sequence, and to give a 'perspective' view of when these events occurred, in relation to the present day. Sequence and time can have self-evident mathematical connections, and where the positions of the events fall on the time line these must be proportional to its length. The idea of proportion is a difficult mathematical concept for young children to grasp, but one that can both be highlighted and made easier by the appropriate use of ICT. Drawing a time line in this way is an opportunity not to be missed.

The ICT work for the suggested ideas in both the geography and history sections could be completed using the drawing tools which come as part of *Microsoft Office*, particularly through the use of *Word* and/or *PowerPoint*. These could be used for both the drawings and the time line, and have the added advantage in that these applications can then be used to present findings to a wide-ranging audience in a number of different ways, either as a *PowerPoint* presentation or for printing out as a word-processed document. This could also include the insertion of clipart and pictures, which would naturally enhance any history or geography work, as well as allowing the children to practise their ICT skills in a meaningful and practical context. If pictures are to be included they could be cut and pasted from various sources, including images taken by the children with a digital or film camera, scans, the Internet and CD-ROMs. When using *PowerPoint*, video clips could also be used, sourced from the Web, CD-ROMs or where the children have made and then edited their own digital videos.

Physical education

Although the National Curriculum for England specifically mentions that ICT is a subject in its own right, it also states that where possible, it should be employed to support teaching and learning in the other curriculum subjects – except for PE. This is a curious omission, for this is arguably the one area of the curriculum that genuinely allows for extensive and completely non-contrived use of ICT. PE also lends itself ideally to the incorporation of mathematics, so the combination of PE, ICT and mathematics offers genuine opportunities for a range of practical activities in a 'real world' context, particularly through the handling data strand.

Children can observe and record a range of data about themselves, especially in a health-related fitness context as part of a wider science investigation. This might include the children taking their pulses after several short bursts of intense physical activity – say five 20-second bench steps – then the results could then be entered into a class spreadsheet and analysed by the children through the posing of key questions, such as:

- 'What is your pulse rate at rest, before activity?'
- 'What is your pulse rate after 20 seconds of intense activity?'
- 'What is your pulse rate after another 20 seconds of intense activity?'
- 'What is your pulse rate after yet another 20 seconds of intense activity?'
- 'What is your pulse rate one minute after activity?'
- 'What is your pulse rate two minutes after activity?'
- 'What is your pulse rate three minutes after activity?'

This then leads to the next obvious question:

- 'What is your average pulse rate?'

The use of a spreadsheet could plot this information as a graph. A graph could illustrate where the pulse rate peaks, and could also illustrate where the pulse rate 'plateaus' and where it steadily declines to a more normal level once the activity is complete.

The results of each member of the class could then be directly compared and contrasted. This would clearly have to be handled sensitively, but some meaningful conclusions could be drawn from the resulting information. The children could be asked to explain the 'shape' of the resulting graph. Why are there peaks and troughs? How do these compare to the actual movements? What would be the appropriate graph to use – a line graph, or a thin bar chart? The children could try both and decide for themselves.

The whole sequences could be recorded by a digital video camera. The children could then edit the moving images using a digital video editing tool such as *iMovie* on the *Apple iMac* computer or *Adobe Premiere* on a personal computer. They could add a voice-over explaining how they felt, or what their pulse was at different points in the activities. If the school does not have this equipment, still images can be captured using a digital still camera or a film camera and scanning the pictures into a computer. The images could be incorporated into a *Microsoft Word* document or a *PowerPoint* slide show, perhaps with screenshots from the spreadsheet, such as *Number Box* or *Microsoft Excel*.

Other data handling activities where ICT and PE could be used to support mathematics might involve recording times from a running race or for measuring distances in long jumping. Like the example above, they could be entered into a spreadsheet and analysed in a number of meaningful ways.

Conclusion

A growing body of evidence based on the experiences of teachers and student teachers supports the claim that already in many schools the curriculum has become lop-sided (Riley and Prentice, 1999). One way of redressing the balance must be to look for areas within subjects that can be taught as an integrated project. This need not result in these subjects being taught in either a shallow or a superficial way. The appropriate use of ICT can be both the 'cement' that holds the project together, and the tool that allows for the subjects to be taught in depth.

Bibliography

Ager, R., *Information and Communications Technology in Primary Schools*, David Fulton Publishers, London, 1998.

Bielby, C., 'Plants and numbers in the classroom', *Primary Science and Technology*, Spring, 2003: 15–17.

Gamble, N. and Easingwood, N. (eds), *ICT and Literacy*, Continuum, London, 2000.

Millwood, R., 'A new relationship with media?', in Gamble, N. and Easingwood, N. (eds), *ICT and Literacy*, Continuum, London, 2000.

Riley, J. and Prentice, R., *The Curriculum for 7–11 Year Olds*, Paul Chapman Publishers, London, 1998.

Watt, D., 'Science: learning to explain how the world works', in Riley, J. and Prentice, R. (eds), *The Curriculum for 7–11 Year Olds*, Paul Chapman Publishers, London, 1999.

Williams, J. and Easingwood, N., *ICT and Primary Science*, RoutledgeFalmer, London, 2003.

For further information on the Science and Plants for Schools project, visit: http://www.saps.org.uk.

Chapter 10

Some ideas for other mathematics and the use of ICT

There are so many areas of mathematics that lend themselves to the good use of ICT that it is difficult to know where to start. It is also surprising that all (or at least most) of school mathematics is currently not done on the computer. This is surprising as mathematics is the one curriculum subject that arguably lends itself to the use of ICT more than any other area of the curriculum. One of the reasons perhaps is that there are just not enough suitable programs, certainly for primary children, and most of what is available seems to fall into the 'drill and practice' category, as described in our chapter on planning. There are of course, the range of programs that give us the databases and spreadsheets, which are described elsewhere in this book. However, there seems to be a dearth of programs that provide an exciting introduction to areas of pure or applied mathematics – could this be one result of the introduction of the National Numeracy Strategy? What we are suggesting in this chapter is that, by making use of existing programs, we can either introduce children to some new ideas in mathematics, or at the very least, teach the existing mathematics in a different way. In both cases the mathematics involves a good and effective use of ICT. In this chapter we will give just three examples of mathematics, and how they can be enhanced by the good use of ICT.

Vectors

Teachers may have often used these without knowing that they have done so. There are many occasions when children are asked to produce lists of numbers, where it is important that these numbers should be in a special order. For example, let us imagine that a class of 24 children are making a monster's tea party for their end-of-year celebrations. Each child will have:

- Two green sweets.
- Three blue cakes.
- One pink biscuit.

This could be written as:

$$\begin{pmatrix} 2 \\ 3 \\ 1 \end{pmatrix}$$

Although there are three different foodstuffs, these will be on each child's plate, and the brackets show us that mathematically we are going to treat them as a single unit, which we shall call a 'column vector'. The numbers are the 'elements' of the vector.

We can multiply vectors, so for instance let us take this example to show how many elements we shall need:

$$24 \times \begin{pmatrix} 2 \\ 3 \\ 1 \end{pmatrix} = \begin{pmatrix} 48 \\ 72 \\ 24 \end{pmatrix}$$

We can also add vectors, but we need to make certain that the numbers in each of the column vectors represent the same things. For instance, if each child also had one plastic knife, a plate and a paper napkin, these could be listed as a column vector:

$$\begin{pmatrix} 1 \\ 1 \\ 1 \end{pmatrix}$$

However, they could not be added to the previous vector to make any sense, because if we tried, the resulting column vector would show a number of things but we wouldn't know if they were knives or green sweets, plates or blue cakes, or napkins or pink biscuits. To add vectors the elements both need to be similar things and at the same time relevant to each other. For example, it obviously would be no use adding children's measurements together – height, hand spans, arm lengths, etc. – since the result would just show one giant child! A better example would be to take the recipe for one of the items of the children's party listed above – the pink biscuits.

- Flour   (grams)
- Sugar   (grams)
- Butter   (grams)
- Eggs   (number)

This can be expressed as a column vector:

$$\begin{pmatrix} 100 \\ 100 \\ 100 \\ 1 \end{pmatrix}$$

This would make about 24 biscuits. Somebody would go shopping for these ingredients. (We shall forget the red food dye for the moment, as one bottle would last you for many more parties, unless you were to use it for other interesting science work.) However, as well as these biscuits you also need to make those blue cakes, which need very similar ingredients – although a different method of mixing them and in different quantities (again, we shall forget the food dye).

- Flour (grams)
- Sugar (grams)
- Butter (grams)
- Eggs (number)

This can also be expressed as a column vector:

$$\begin{pmatrix} 600 \\ 300 \\ 300 \\ 2 \end{pmatrix}$$

Because these ingredients are the same you can go shopping for the lot, and, mathematically, you can safely add these vectors together:

	Biscuit	Cake	Total
Flour (grams)	100	600	700
Sugar (grams)	100	300	400
Butter (grams)	100	300	400
Eggs (number)	1	2	3

If you were to look up the definition of a vector in a mathematical dictionary the chances are that it would involve direction, movement, and a considerable amount of geometry. If you looked it up in an ordinary dictionary it would likely as not define it only as a direction. Hence the definition and, once the basic idea is understood, vectors can indeed help us understand many aspects of geometry, as well as applied mechanics and higher physics. Although the authors hope that readers are or will become interested in the mathematics included in this book for its own sake, it is not meant to be a mathematical text, so we leave it to the readers to decide if they want more. They may well be interested to find out how vectors can illustrate and explain aspects of forces and velocities, although from a primary maths point of view it would be better to stay with directional and distance vectors.

If you were to ask a child in your class to go out of one door and walk 10 paces, and ask a second child also to walk 10 paces, but this time from a different door, then they would obviously end up in two very different places. One might have gone north 10 paces, the other east for 10 paces. If you wanted them to end up at the same spot you would need to fix a point – a co-ordinate. Teachers will be very aware of this aspect of mathematics. They will have taught the children simple co-ordinates on squared paper, and would have reinforced this knowledge with paper-and-pencil games such as Battleships or Treasure Island. Older children will have used co-ordinates with maps and charts. However, once you use these co-ordinates to plan a journey from one place or landmark to another you can soon find yourself involved with vectors. We could plot a journey just by giving the children a set of co-ordinates. They could then decide for themselves how and in which direction they should travel to get from one co-ordinate to another. A simple list of co-ordinates will not tell them. They may have a map and take the first two co-ordinates on the list, and trace a straight line between them with the idea that they should follow this. However, if this line turned out to be a direction on a map which took them into a swamp, they would need to travel in one direction for a certain distance, change direction to circumnavigate the swamp, then finally travel for another set distance to reach their second co-ordinate. Mathematics has many examples of lengths that are measured in directions. These journeys are but one example of many, and can easily be represented mathematically on paper, using the same notation as that given above for the monster's tea party.

Let us take a piece of squared paper, and for the example that follows take one square as one unit (on a map it could represent any given length). We can pick anywhere as a starting point, but for this example the bottom left-hand corner will do (see Figure 10.1). We want to reach a point five squares along and six squares up as a co-ordinate (5,6). The direction would be drawn as a line from the corner to this point – in geographical terms, a little north of north-east (some good cross-curricular work here). However, a direct line takes us through a swamp. To avoid this we shall go two squares along and two up. Then we will go two squares along and none up, and then one square along and four up. (For mathematical vectors we do not normally use compass directions, but we will include them in this example to help the reader to follow the journey.)

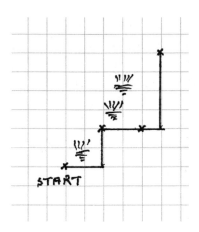

Figure 10.1 The instructions to get from one point to another, avoiding the swamp, drawn on squared paper.

This journey can be written as vectors like this:

$$\begin{pmatrix} 2 \\ 2 \end{pmatrix} + \begin{pmatrix} 2 \\ 0 \end{pmatrix} + \begin{pmatrix} 1 \\ 4 \end{pmatrix} = \begin{pmatrix} 5 \\ 6 \end{pmatrix}$$

It could also have been written:

$$\begin{pmatrix} 2 \\ 2 \end{pmatrix} + \begin{pmatrix} 3 \\ 4 \end{pmatrix}$$

The final vector which is the sum of the three vectors, is of course the original co-ordinate to which the children were asked to travel. However, this journey is solely represented as a mathematical equation.

So far our vector journey has always been in two directions – to the right (or east) and either directly upwards (or north) or diagonally upwards (about north-east). However, with vectors we can also travel in other directions. If we take any point on a grid – say (5,5) – and want to go down to (7,3), then we travel two squares to the right (east), but two squares down (south – the journey will be in a south-easterly direction). This can be mathematically represented by a minus number for the latter two squares:

$$\begin{pmatrix} 2 \\ -2 \end{pmatrix}$$

Similarly, if we want to travel from right to left in a westerly direction, we use a minus number. If we travel downwards at the same time then both numbers will be minus quantities. In other words, on our squared paper, if ever the vector journey takes us backwards or downwards we use a minus number.

A journey from co-ordinate (6,5) to (0,0) (the corner of the grid, or 0 on the x and y axis whichever you prefer), through co-ordinates (3,3) and (3,1), will look like this written in vectors:

$$\begin{pmatrix} 6 \\ 5 \end{pmatrix} + \begin{pmatrix} -3 \\ -2 \end{pmatrix} + \begin{pmatrix} 0 \\ -2 \end{pmatrix} + \begin{pmatrix} -3 \\ -1 \end{pmatrix}$$

Added together they come to $\begin{pmatrix} 0 \\ 0 \end{pmatrix}$ which is, of course, the 'corner' of the grid (see Figure 10.2).

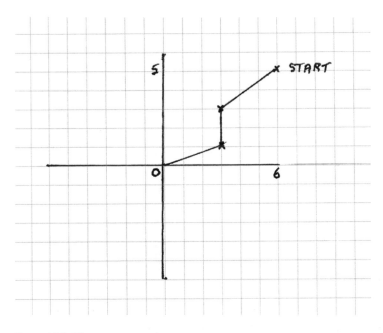

Figure 10.2 The journey to the zero point.

We should remember that we can also go backwards from right to left, which will be in a minus direction, but at the same time upwards in a positive direction. Hence a move from co-ordinate (4,4) to (1,5) will read as vector

$\begin{pmatrix} -3 \\ 1 \end{pmatrix}$ as shown in Figure 10.3.

There is of course no reason why any mathematics that can be written on paper can't also be written on the screen of a computer. However, using the computer to calculate and draw these co-ordinates and vectors on a screen gives an

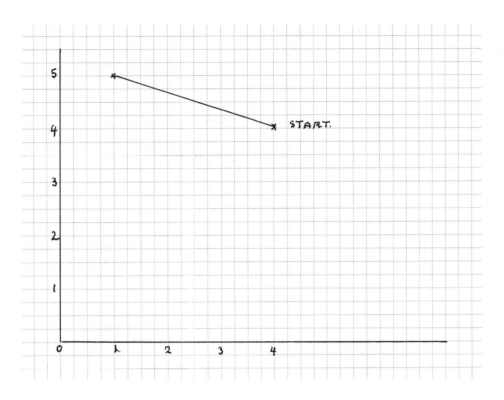

Figure 10.3 The journey from right to left. This is not a line graph: it is a vector journey drawn on a grid. We have enlarged this one so that each unit is 4-by-4 small squares.

immediacy to the mathematics, that brings a whole new dimension to the process of learning.

Sets, mappings and relations

Teachers will be familiar with much of the work to do with sets, mappings and relations, but it is possible that they will not always recognise the connections between them. Nearly all arithmetic and algebra is centred on 'relationships', and indeed we have even heard it said that mathematics is all about relations – relations between numbers, between shapes, between sets of objects, relations between points on a graph and so on. Be that as it may, the mapping of one set to another can often clarify what may be at first glance an insuperable mathematical conundrum. Teachers need to understand, of course, that as with vectors (described above), what we describe here is only the beginnings of a mathematical operation. In the primary school we teach the processes of mapping as a tool for other learning. Hence we might use it to reinforce and motivate. For example, we might start at Key Stage 1 by mapping the relationship between a set of children to a set of months in the year, with the relationship being 'has a birthday in the month of'. This is illustrated by Figure 10.4. However, a more strictly mathematical example suitable for this age, where each member of one set is exactly related to a member of the other set, would be two sets with the relation 'has had 7 added to it'. This is illustrated by Figure 10.5.

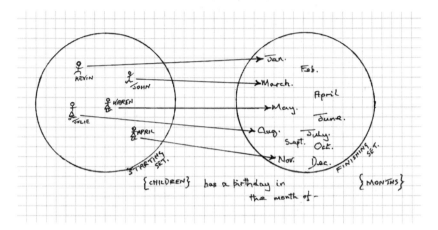

Figure 10.4 Sets showing relationships between children and their birthdays.

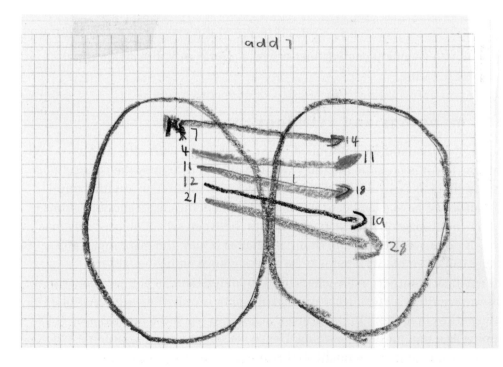

Figure 10.5 An actual example of children's work, where 7 has been added to each number.

However, by Year 6 children could well be completing both one-to-one and many-to-one mappings of a strictly mathematical kind. Figures 10.6 and 10.7 show two such examples.

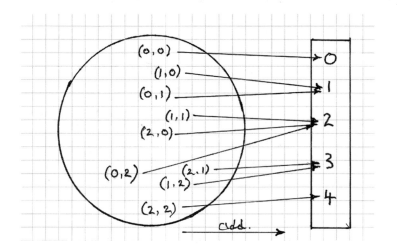

Figure 10.6 Mapping the addition of {0, 1, 2}.

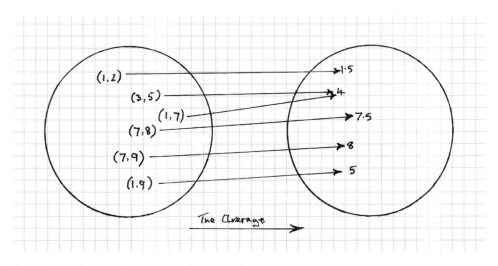

Figure 10.7 Mapping the average of two numbers.

We have described in a previous chapter how many of the graphs that children draw are functions in that they relate one value or fact on the horizontal axis to another on the vertical. We could, perhaps, just as well have made a simple graph of the birthday mapping (Figure 10.4). Perhaps, then, another question we should ask the children (and ourselves) when considering a graphical representation, is: 'Could this information be better displayed as a mapping?'

Loci

One of the dangers that we must guard against when introducing relatively advanced concepts to children is oversimplification. This is not only patronising to the children, but is poor mathematics. If the concept cannot be described in a way that is within the children's experience, and 'concrete' practical, everyday examples are not appropriate, then it is better not to teach it at all. However, if the above conditions are met, then loci, particularly with the help of a computer, is an area of mathematics that can be shown, even to primary school children.

In textbooks, a locus is often described as a set of points that satisfy certain strict conditions. Yet, it is surprising how many of these books never seem to explain what these conditions are. The points could well be a set of numbered pairs plotted on a graph. The resulting curve or straight line (depending on what graph is being drawn) could be thought of as the locus of the points – in other words, the geometric equivalent of the graph's related pairs. This, however, may be too abstract at this stage. What is important is that we show that, whilst a set of points on a plane (the loci) can be described mathematically, for young children it is mechanical examples that are required. In our chapter about the use of graphs, one example of the line graphs was a parabola. This can be described mathematically as the shape obtained on a graph by plotting the equation $y = x^2$. In that chapter, its drawing was described in a practical way, yet within a mathematical context. Parabolas have certain well-defined properties that allow them to be used for many everyday things. Television and radar dish receivers are based on parabolic curves, as are the reflectors of electric fires and car headlights. The water in a fountain as it begins to fall to earth describes a parabola, as does the stream of water from a garden hose. This can easily be shown to children in the school grounds. As long as they can get a good view of the water, perhaps by sitting down, they will see the parabola formed as the water leaves the hose. If this stream of water can be broken up by continually turning the water on and off, then these squirts of water can be thought of as locus points, illustrated in a mechanical way.

An even more practical example of loci, although for reasons of safety one best done as a diagram, is to follow the path of a vehicle. We have all had to move aside when a large lorry turns a corner, and we can often see in towns signs of damage where the lorry has not quite succeeded. Figure 10.8 shows the plan view of such a lorry, with its front wheels turned but its rear wheels straight. With a series of joined-up dots, the first one being on the top of each wheel, we can trace the path of the turning vehicle. If we place a dot at each corner of the lorry we can trace its turning circle, which will be different for the front and

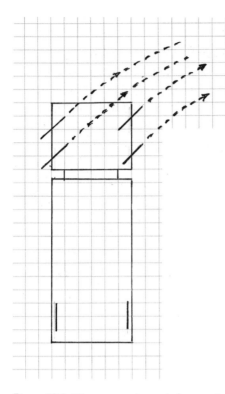

Figure 10.8 Diagram to show the approximate path taken by the front wheels of the lorry. What path would the rear wheels take? Where would it be safe to stand?

back of the vehicle. We could also try this with a plan of a large articulated lorry. Used in this way, we can also define a locus as being the path of an object, in this case any point on the lorry, moving in a specific way.

The paths shown In Figure 10.8 have regular shapes because in this case there are wheels and axles that can be directed by the driver, and they move in a given direction. In other words, the set of points, because it is well defined, can be joined together in a predictable way. However, there are examples in nature that we can use that may at first glance, appear to be random. If we follow the movements of a small animal such as an insect or a wood louse we can make a plot of its journey, just as we drew the movements of the lorry. However, these movements would be far from predictable, so it would not be until we had carried out the exercise, and carefully highlighted a set of points, that we could say exactly what the locus was. This might be shown on the screen by using the screen turtle as a model insect, as described in the LOGO chapters.

Using the computer

Vectors

These examples of vector journeys were produced using the drawing tools of *Microsoft Word*. This was done by ensuring that the 'Drawing' toolbar was present at the foot of the screen, then clicking on the word 'Draw'. 'Grid' was then selected and a grid of one centimetre squares constructed. The line tool was then used to draw the straight line between the two chosen points where the gridlines intersect, and the line was then widened to size 3 point for clarity (Figures 10.9 to 10.12). The vectors were written using a piece of software called *Equation*, which comes as part of *Microsoft Office*. This program contains a large number of mathematical symbols and notations, and allows the user to write mathematical formulae, equations and, in this case, to create vectors. These are then copied and pasted into the appropriate position in a similar way to a picture. This could also be achieved by using the interactive whiteboard and selecting the squared paper tile background.

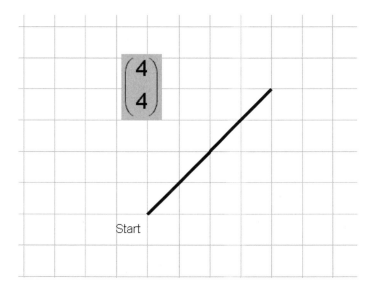

Figure 10.9 A simple diagonal vector drawn from left to right.

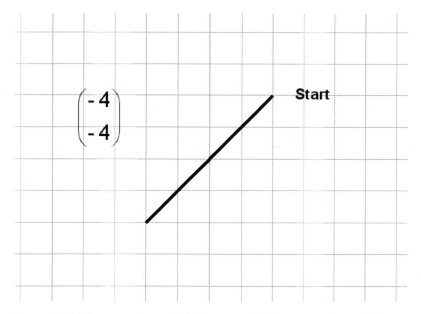

Figure 10.10 This vector line, although apparently the same as Figure 10.9, starts at the top and travels downwards and to the left, hence the minus numbers.

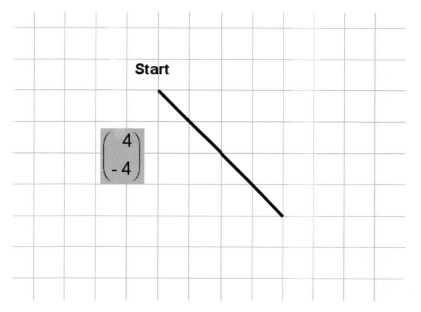

Figure 10.11 The same journey, but this time travelling downwards and to the right.

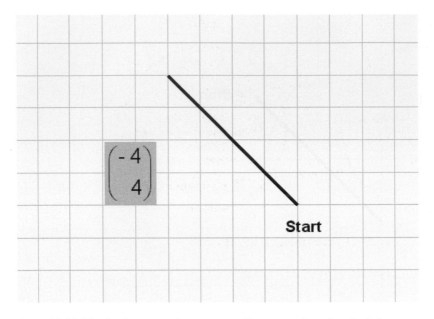

Figure 10.12 The final journey, this time travelling upwards and to the left.

Sets and mappings

The drawing tools of *Microsoft Word* can also be used to produce drawings for sets and mappings. On this occasion the circle icon is selected on the drawing toolbar and is then dragged onto the screen to form a circle. When the user is happy with the size and position on the page, the second circle is created by copying and pasting the first circle into the desired position. This ensures that the second circle is the same size as the first. The required words or numbers are then typed into the circles, but it is necessary first to select 'Text wrapping' from the 'Picture' toolbar, with the 'Behind text' option being selected. This will allow the text to be positioned in what appear to be the circles. The text is in fact in a layer above the level of the circle, and if the circle is not placed behind the text it will not be visible. The arrows are selected from the 'Drawing' toolbar and are drawn into the required positions, and are then widened using the appropriate icon (Figure 10.13).

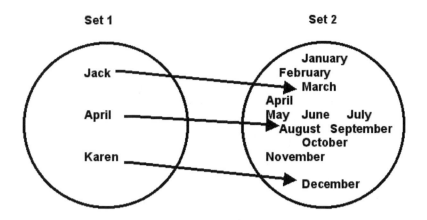

Has a birthday in the month of -

Figure 10.13 Simple mapping similar to Figure 10. 4.

Loci

Once again, the drawing tools of *Microsoft Word* were utilised, producing Figure 10.14. A similar grid to that used for the vectors illustrated earlier was used as a background. The car was drawn by creating a 3-square-by-4-square rectangle, which was then filled. The wheels were drawn by creating one small rectangle, which was then filled with black, copied and pasted a further three times and dragged each time into the required position. The front wheels were turned through approximately 45 degrees by selecting them individually, and then clicking on the 'Free rotate' tool near the left-hand end of the 'Drawing' toolbar. A series of 'handles' appear on each corner of the shape, and these are dragged through the desired angle. The paths of the wheels were drawn by using the 'Curve' line tool. Once one path had been completed, which takes a little practice, this can be copied and pasted onto the other wheel to make a matching pair. It should be noted that we use the word 'path' because we are showing how each point (in this case wheels) will progress.

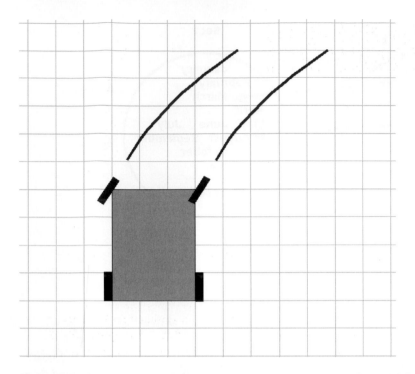

Figure 10.14 The path of a car's front wheels similar to the lorry in Figure 10.8. What do you think the paths of the rear wheels would be?

Conclusion

This chapter has shown that a wide variety of mathematical topics can not only be taught to primary children, but by using standard, commonly available software, can be delivered in a number of interesting and imaginative ways.

Index